Spiritual
Metamorphosis
Volume 2

Spiritual Metamorphosis Volume 2

Gate by Gate

Ralph Riley

This publication is meant as a source of valuable information for the reader, however it is not meant as a substitute for direct expert assistance. If such level of assistance is required, the services of a competent professional should be sought.

Copyright © 2024 by Ralph Riley

All rights reserved. No part of this book may be reproduced or transmitted in any form or by any means, electronic or mechanical, including photocopying, recording, or any information storage and retrieval system, without permission in writing from the author.

ISBN: 978-1-6653-0865-6 - Paperback
eISBN: 978-1-6653-0866-3 - eBook

These ISBNs are the property of BookLogix for the express purpose of sales and distribution of this title. The content of this book is the property of the copyright holder only. BookLogix does not hold any ownership of the content of this book and is not liable in any way for the materials contained within. The views and opinions expressed in this book are the property of the Author/Copyright holder, and do not necessarily reflect those of BookLogix.

Library of Congress Control Number: 2023906638

⊚This paper meets the requirements of ANSI/NISO Z39.48-1992 (Permanence of Paper)

Scripture quotations are taken from the Holy Bible, King James Version (Public Domain).

0 7 2 2 2 4

I dedicate this book to my steadfast parents: Mr. Jessie Riley and Dinah Mae Riley of Live Oak, Florida. Their prayers and constant love toward everyone they met provided an example of humility and set the path of the righteousness of God to dwell for their children.

Without their prayers and constant praise and worship, the alternative of life for me and my siblings could have been very different. Thank you, God, for my parents and their love toward you and their children.

One important key to success is self-confidence.
An important key to self-confidence is preparation.

—Arthur Ashe

Contents

Introduction ix

Chapter 4: Adult Phase

Adult Butterfly Ready for Reproduction:	
The Water Gate	1
The Water Gate	4
The Water Gate Experience	7
Spiritual Growth	19
Adult Butterfly Ready for Spiritual Warfare:	
The Horse Gate	21
The Horse Gate	22
The Horse Gate Experience	25
Spiritual Growth	41
Making Disciples of Jesus Christ:	
The East Gate	46
The East Gate	48
The East Gate Experience	52
Spiritual Growth	66
The Inspection Gate: Gathering	
of the Redeemer and the Redeemed	73
Appearance of the	
Bridegroom (Jesus Christ)	81
Day of Consummation for Believers	83
God's Concerns for the Church (Bride)	86
Spiritual Growth	95

Acknowledgments *101*

Introduction

In the book titled *Spiritual Metamorphosis Gate by Gate, Volume 1*, the author discusses the parallel of the caterpillar to the butterfly and the born-again believer to adulthood through the first three phases of the metamorphosis process (transformation).

I pray that the readers were able to identify their spiritual maturity level with the words of exaltation at each phase, and appropriate gates. As mentioned in the introduction of volume 1, the intent was to provide biblical truth without quoting scripture to establish a spiritual processing map to provide levels of spiritual maturity in the believer's faith walk with God.

The word "metamorphosis" is to change from an immature form to an adult form completely different in nature. The book *Spiritual Metamorphosis, Volume 1* is great news; however, the believer is charged to move on to perfection in Christ. The parallel of the caterpillar to the butterfly and the born-again believer is accomplished at this point of the process and the believer is endowed with the basic oracles of the gospel of Jesus Christ. The believer has experienced the Sheep, Fish, Old, Valley, Dung, and Fountain Gates as part of the first three phases of the spiritual metamorphosis.

This book (volume 2) is designed to continue in the gospel of Jesus the Christ to perfection, to be prepared at the Inspection Gate. This book will use Nehemiah's gates, from the Water Gate to the Inspection Gate, to help identify one's spiritual maturity level beyond the change in nature from the first three phases of the metamorphosis. Additionally, this book will assist with the preparation of the believer's spiritual readiness to rejoice at Jesus's return for His church.

Just to recap the process of spiritual metamorphosis discussed in the first three phases, the starting point is the Sheep Gate. The Sheep Gate is preeminent, and believers must enter the Sheep Gate to receive their "badge of salvation" by the grace of God, through Faith in Jesus Christ. There is no other avenue (gate) by which mankind can be saved (delivered from the penalty and bondage of their sin). In the Sheep Gate, the believer experiences the teaching/doctrine of Jesus Christ come alive in the believer's heart, enabling the believer to exercise their Faith in Jesus Christ.

The Sheep Gate is open because of the sacrificial lamb of God, who takes away the sins of the world. Jesus Christ is the *only* door to the Sheep Gate, for anyone who chooses to see the Kingdom of God must enter. The Sheep Gate is the fulfillment of the prophecy of the first coming of Jesus Christ. Jesus told his disciples, "I tell you the truth, I am the gate for the sheep." The Sheep Gate is one of the gates that the builders did not place bolts or bars on to keep others out. Salvation is a free gift by God's grace to whomsoever enters the Sheep Gate. Jesus's death, burial, and resurrection opened the *only* way for mankind to restore access to God the Father.

After the Sheep Gate experience, believers will begin to voice the gospel of Jesus Christ in the Fish Gate (evangelize) to whomsoever God has placed in their path consciously or unconsciously. The Fish Gate experience has provided a new heart and new spirit for the love of mankind propelled by the love of God and his purpose. This histogenesis (the gifts of God before the foundation of the world) in the spirit of the believer is made without hands, in the putting off the body of sins of the flesh. This is the place where the believer begins evangelizing God's presence in their lives experiencing the change in nature.

The Old Gate speaks of a God that changes not. The Old Gate speaks to the change nature of the believer's old man. Unlike the repair of the Old Gate, the believer is not repaired but made anew, killing the deeds of the old fleshly man. This is the season when the love of God and the work of the Holy Spirit restrain the believer, leading them into the righteousness of God. The indwelling Spirit of God enables the believer to deny self the temptation of the world's desires. Through the work of the Holy Spirit and sanctification received by faith, Jesus has set up "bolts and locks" to keep sin from having any rights or authority over the believer. It is the Holy Spirit that kills the deeds of our flesh through obedience of the gospel. The more obedience to the gospel, the less the flesh is tempted. Spiritual growth requires the Old Gate experience to die for self through the power of the Holy Spirit so that the believer can submerge themselves in the will of God for their lives.

The Valley Gate experience has proved to be essential to establishing a relationship with God in a special and customized way designed and orchestrated by God. In the Valley Gate, believers will experience still waters and green pastures because the Chief Shepherd is eminent. Believers that have completed the Valley Gate will seek to enroll in the Dung Gate for spiritual cleansing to go before a holy God.

The Dung Gate is where the action of love through an intimate relationship with God is expressed in a "spirit of gratitude." The fight to cast down imaginations and everything that exalts itself against the knowledge of God is doable with the Holy Spirit.

The Dung Gate is having a naked and unashamed experience in preparation for holiness. Believers must understand that standing before God requires clean hands and a pure heart. This is the phase of the complete metamorphosis that believers no longer approach God in their former depravity status, but through their declared newness of life. While in the Dung Gate, believers through the help of the indwelling Spirit of God begin reordering their priorities in life. Believers change their ways and intent to please God, acknowledging Him in all that they do. This is the season the believer may experience water baptism or understand the precept of water baptism as it pertains to the circumcision of their mind. The believer begins their newness of life through repentance, forgiveness, and faith in Jesus Christ. In the Dung Gate, believers lay aside every weight that is not rooted (dead works, religious rituals) in the faith of Jesus Christ.

While in the Fountain Gate, believers filled with the Holy Spirit experience God using their bodies, soul, and minds as living sacrifices. The first three phases of the metamorphosis surround themselves with the gospel of Jesus Christ to include the teaching of eternal life. The Fountain Gate is where the living water (filling of the Holy Spirit), with or without the believer's consciousness, is expressed without compromising. Believers who are filled with the Holy Spirit and/or anointed (ability to remove burden and yokes) by God have been energized and motivated to feast on the word of God. The filling of the Holy Spirit (gift of God) is where purpose and the anointing of God are merged to execute the ministry of reconciliation. This is the phase when believers become joint occupants in the body of Christ in preparation for Jesus's return. The Fountain Gate is the place where believers become living sacrifices for the gospel of Jesus Christ and the expansion of the Kingdom of God.

This book will move the believer from the Fountain Gate with anointing and power from on high through the Water Gate to the Inspection Gate. This book will encourage the believer to meditate on the word of God, day and night for instructions and guidance. These instructions will provide insight into the enemy's plot and the spiritual weaponry designed to ward off his attack(s).

In the book of Romans (Book of Righteousness), the author Apostle Paul provides practical exhortation as it pertains to service and duties of the believer in the body of Christ. In chapter 12, Paul explains the responsibilities of believers toward God and toward society. Paul, through the inspiration of God, explains the duties and spiritual positions for believers to walk under the influence of the indwelling Holy Spirit. These instructions will require the believer's body, mind, and soul to yield to the voice of the word of God. It is the body of the believer that carries out what is conceived in the mind. The believer's confession of sin, their willingness to obey the commandment of God, is insufficient to carry out God's plan and purpose for their lives. Believers are charged to yield their spiritual and physical member as members of the body of Christ with dedication as living sacrifices for the service of God. Therefore, Paul is instructing believers to be transformed and not be conformed to the trends and fashion of this world's culture.

Chapter 4

Adult Phase

Adult Butterfly Ready for Reproduction: The Water Gate

Adulthood of the butterfly is the phase after pupating for reproduction to further glorify God with their awesome beauty. After pupation, the adult butterfly searches for a mate of the same species to produce viable offspring to carry on their genes. Butterflies must feast on their host plants, the plant from which they started the metamorphosis. The host plant (true light) is vital to the butterfly's ability to reproduce. Artificial light can impede the processes responsible for the butterfly's navigational ability to fly.

Likewise, the believer is to search out mates

(partner, companion) to expand the Kingdom of God. Unlike the butterfly, this search for a mate is not limited to the same fold nor to producing viable offspring to continue the genes of physical birth but searching the highways and byways for those separated from God for spiritual birth. This spiritual birth is fulfilling the commandment of God to go into all the world and preach the gospel of Jesus Christ to all creation. This is the phase of maturity where the indwelling Spirit of God is confirming God's word with signs and wonders.

Liken unto the butterfly, it is vital that the believer feast on the word of God as their host plant (true light) from which they started their spiritual metamorphosis. The word of God will always be the catalyst (agent that provokes change) to the beginning and the ending of the believer's faith. The complete nature change will require the believer to meditate day and night on the host plant.

Liken unto the butterfly, artificial light (false teaching) can impede the believer's mission to expand the Kingdom of God. The believer's navigational system (mind) will require spiritual renewing changes for a spiritual purpose. False teaching can impede the believer's mission to take on the ministry of reconciliation. The word of God is the truth, and everything outside of the word of God is artificial.

This is the mature phase of the metamorphosis where the believer begins living by the truth of God's word that causes light to shine in a dark place. The word of God is designed to open the believer's eyes from darkness to the spiritual light of knowledge and wisdom. This is the light that will expose what is hidden in darkness. This is the light that will expose the intent and motives of the god of this world and his attempt to kill, steal, and destroy the believer's good works. The word of God is the light that reveals the gospel of Jesus Christ that displays the glory of Christ, who is the image of God.

The word of God warns against artificial light of false doctrine that can hinder the believer's empowerment over the god of this world. This is the phase of the metamorphosis where the artificial light of emotional highs, and itching ears that appease the flesh, can no longer be accepted, and received by the believer. This is the maturity level where believers renew their mind with the truth of God's word. Without the spiritual light of the word of God, believers cannot discern or know the will of God to act as ambassadors of Jesus Christ. This is level of maturity that is paramount and vital to the believer's salvation and the expansion of the Kingdom of God. This is the phase when the believers avoid the traps and snares of the enemies due to lack of knowledge. This is the phase of maturity that believers' desires are to be lost in the shadows of Jesus the Christ.

The Water Gate

The Water Gate reminds believers of the word of God. The word of God has cleansing and renewing power to cause change, and deliverance. The Water Gate is recorded in history as having no need to be repaired, as the word of God is sovereign (possessing supreme power), having no need for outside sources, and will never fail. The word of God is settled in heaven!

The Water Gate is where the word of God is acknowledged as the source of life, as the source of strength in the face of tumult and confusion, as the anchor to the believer's soul (relied on for support, stability, or security). The Water Gate is the will of God for the believer's light in life and will simplify and amplify the covenant union between Christ and the believer. Whether the believer is filled with the Holy Spirit or not, the Water Gate is the power of God unto deliverance (Salvation) to all who have ears to hear what the Spirit of the Lord is saying. The Water Gate is one of the two gates associated with the building of the walls of Jerusalem, said to have no need of repairing. John the Baptist read and taught the law of God to the people of God at this gate. This is the gate where the truth is being taught by God's ambassadors (messengers) to his people. The Water Gate is the source of truth to prepare the people to come before a holy God. The Water Gate is settled in heaven and uninjured by the world and its systems. The word of God is the only "cleansing power" prescribed for the washing and purification of believers.

This adult phase will bring the believer to a place where they are barren before God within their own resources, understanding God's grace is perfected in their weakness. The Water Gate experience will prompt believers to become naked and not unashamed before God and mankind. The Water Gate will propel the believer to change their narrative to glorify God in everything they do. This is the place where the word of God changes the believer's narrative to one seasoned with salt, edifying to all those that God has placed in their care Gate by Gate. This is the season when glorification is revealed. This is the season when the adult believers come to the end of the final phase and application of their redemption.

This is the gate where the word of God, after the pupation of the believer's nature, now mirrors the image of Jesus the Christ. This is the gate where divine purpose to glorify God is demonstrated through unwavering faith, and boldness that Christ will be exalted in the body of the believer. This is the gate where God receives the proper reverence, respect, honor, and majesty from the believer because of who HE is. This is the gate where believers receive revelation knowledge of their rights in the Kingdom of God, where believers receive the righteousness of God through faith. This is the gate where glorification takes on new meaning identifying the believer as a vessel of honor to expand the Kingdom of God.

Without the Water Gate, the believer's faith is limited and can never become the amen of the word of God. Believers meditating on the word of God to show themselves approval will produce the fruit of the Holy Spirit for confirmation of God's love for mankind. Believers who engage in the search for the revelation knowledge of God will discover the image of Jesus Christ (Son of Man) to be one of friendliness and approachability. The Water Gate will require meditation in the word of God giving the believer "power of attorney" to act on God's behalf. The Water Gate will propel the believer to be driven by the Holy Spirit to speak on God's behalf without a measure of power, perfecting the love of God. The Water Gate is the phase of the adulthood of the metamorphosis where believers create a temple (spirit of the believer) that God can dwell in. This is the phase when the believer's covenant with

God provides mankind access to God for eternal life.

Remember, God foreknew the events and the whereabouts of the believer's journey and has provided provisions for their escape and blessing for their cause. When we as believers know that God is with us, we as believers are as bold as a lion. This is the gate where the believer repents of their sinful acts and fights for the consequences of the love of God, fights for their great salvation and promises of God as a good soldier.

The Water Gate Experience

This level of spiritual maturity will require a love for God that equals the likeness of God (His nature) and beyond the image of Christ (visible representation). This kind of love goes beyond the dating game with God, beyond the visible representation of Christ. The anointing of the Holy Spirit will provide the power and authority to bring forth fruit, but the execution of God's will, will rest on the believer's love for God. This level of maturity requires holiness (full agreement with God), humility, and Jesus as Lord to the believer. This level of holiness will deepen the believer's love and gratitude for the grace God extended through the work of Jesus Christ on the cross. When the believer is engulfed in holiness, the believer's lifestyle reflects the character of God for all of mankind to witness. The more the word of God shapes the believer's heart through sacrifice, habits, and obedience, the more the believer puts away childish things because of their love for God.

The believer's daily cleansing and washing by the word of God perfecting holiness will lead to the fear (reverence) of God for change. This is the place where the believer's disposition toward the will of God is supported through aligning themselves to the word of God to act as ambassadors of Christ. This is the place believers provide a visual representation that shows forth the image of Christ. This is the place believers began to work closely with the Holy Spirit to receive the spirit of discernment (gift of God to see or hear the intent of something from God's perspective).

This is the phase of spiritual maturity when believers understand that the word of God is filled with all the necessary ingredients (the covenant and union between God and the believer) and nutrients (joy of the Lord that promotes spiritual growth and maintains life) pertaining to life, and godliness from God, who has called them to glory and virtue. It is not the lack of spiritual knowledge that hinders the believer's communion with God, but their mindset toward their gratitude for God's grace and love that has brought them to this phase of their spiritual maturity.

As believers study the word of God to show themselves approval, their spiritual knowledge will raise their standard of conduct, making spiritual experiences clearly visible. This experience will change the believer's ability to further obey God from faith to faith through the working of the Holy Spirit. The word of God is the seed (food source) for spiritual growth, fitting for spiritual reproduction. Therefore, believers are to be renewed in the spirit of their minds with the word of God that they might be a suitable helpmeet for God and his purpose. The world is waiting on the sons and daughters of God to show forth God's grace and power for deliverance. The world is hurting, and the constant changing culture and its fashions are setting precedent that God is not real, and the gospel of Jesus Christ cannot be the resolve.

The word of God is not only the anchor to the soul of the believer, but also provides the strength, energy, and power to deny one's self the temptations of this world and the lust after fleshly desires. When believers stand on the word of God as a lifeline with hope to rejoice in the day of Jesus's return, their labor and service to God have not been in vain.

The Water Gate is where the love of God (word of

God) will not impute judgment toward the believer's unrighteous acts but will hold judgment in the balance (right standing with God after repentance) until sanctification (the presence of sin) has fully come in Jesus's presence.

Ministry of Reconciliation

This phase of spiritual maturity is taking on the ministry of reconciliation. Believers tell the story that regardless of one's circumstances or conditions, mankind can have a relationship with God through Jesus Christ. Believers acting under the authority and voice of the indwelling Spirit of God will be challenged regarding their knowledge and faith in God's word. This is the place where believers return to the Fish Gate experience with compassion and empathy for the ignorance of the grace of God (those that are lost).

The ministry of reconciliation explains the end of an estrangement between mankind's spiritual Father, caused by sin, and the grace of God, accessed through faith in Jesus Christ. Today and every day, the Sheep Gate is open so that mankind can end their spiritual orphan status. The ministry of reconciliation empowers the believer to tell the story that Jesus is standing at the door of mankind's heart knocking with a bouquet of love. The question remains constant: Who will tell them that Jesus loves them? Who will tell them there is a better way?

The Water Gate is the place where believers receive the ministry of reconciliation as laborers of God into a harvest of lost souls. It is through the ministry of reconciliation the lost can establish an intimate relationship with God through faith in Jesus Christ. The Water Gate is the place where believers are sent by God and anointed with power to declare the message of the gospel of Jesus Christ. This is the place where the believer takes on the challenge to spread the new covenant, permitting the ministry of reconciliation to be a voluntary service in their lives.

This is the place and time believers relish the opportunity to share the gospel (preached) to the poor in spirit, the brokenhearted, those in captivity and bondage of this world's system. This is a place and season believers declare the message of restoration with God through faith in Jesus Christ. This faith and proclamation of the good news (gospel) and its assurance of forgiveness of sin is the work of Jesus on the cross. This forgiveness of sin is available to whomsoever will believe.

In the Water Gate, believers become familiar with their part of God's restoration plan through the prompting of the indwelling Spirit of God. Many times, as believers, our responsibility is to just plant the seed or water the seed, understanding that it is God who gives the increase. Believers must be careful to obey the voice of the Spirit of God to avoid any consequences that can frustrate the matter and delay the seed from bringing forth good fruit. This message of reconciliation is God's will and plan for the expansion of the Kingdom of God.

We live in a season when the people of this world are crying out, "No man cares for my soul," as refugees (outcasts) of this now culture that has failed them. Mankind is seeking refuge in their jobs and in their community, looking for the sons and daughters of God to recognize their identity, to recognize their pain and bondage for help. We now live in a culture that has ignored the only antidote to life (blood of Jesus). The harvest is plentiful of those alienated from their spiritual Father, spiritual orphans in a world with a mindset that no one cares about their souls.

The people of this world without a relationship with God are screaming from the mountaintops and from the streets, literally begging and asking earnestly for deliverance. The world is seeking help from anyone that will release them from their captivity, those on death row without God in this world. Without the wisdom and understanding of the word of God, believers are merely believers (soldiers) in the reserves waiting on a call for deployment that has already been issued via the word of God (Water Gate). As sons and daughters of God believers are charged to stand in the gap and cause change as agents (force) and ambassadors of Christ. Without ambassadors of Christ and spiritual agents, mankind will perish and cannot escape the reality of this dark world. The world is seeking the sons and daughters of God for refuge. If believers fail to renew their minds with the word of God, the poor in spirit will continue to remain hidden in caves and catacombs enduring the weight of sin upon their shoulders, thinking no man cares for their souls.

Renewed Mind

The greatest need of mankind is a renewed mind. The old way of thinking has only caused separation from God and His righteousness. A renewed mind is required to fully glorify God as a living sacrifice. A renewed mind is required to ensure holiness (set apart for God's use) and to fulfill the covenant agreement to go preach the gospel to all the world. Holiness demands that followers of Christ (those that fit the description as sons and daughters of God) strive to overcome evil with good, to reach the measure of maturity of adulthood with the ability to reproduce the likeness of God and the image of Jesus Christ.

Walking in the Spirit of a renewed mind relieves the believer of obligations to ensure the word of God spoken from their heart comes to pass. The believer is simply an instrument, and the power and authority for results and desired spiritual side effects of the spoken word depends on the power of God. There should be some desired side effects of the word of God and union with the Holy Spirit that demonstrate the image of Christ. These side effects are not the proof of the believer's power, but proof of the Holy Spirit working in God's will.

The Water Gate is where the believer renews the spirit of their mind with the word of God to walk in their newness of life after the image of Jesus Christ in true righteousness and holiness. The believer is no longer righteous in their own mind and way of thinking. A renewed mind will move the believer from faith to faith, continuing the lifelong battle of the mind to put off the old nature and put on the new nature based on the word of God. The more the believer entangles themselves with the word of God, as their breath of life depends on it, the more the believer's heart is established blameless in holiness before God. Mankind's soul cannot rest until the believer's mind becomes renewed with the word of God and the ministry of reconciliation is accepted and executed. This is the phase when the "engrafted" word (living extension of one's life) of God impregnates the believer, causing side effects to obey the word of God without hesitation.

This is the season when the believer's laboring in the word of God is not used for intellectual conversations, but to understand how to worship God in excellence. It is the word of God that brings holiness (God's separateness and uniqueness) to completion in the fear of God, working out one's own salvation. The believer's mindset prior to engaging in prayer, praise, or worship is vital to the appropriate fear level of God to gain communion that produces desired fruit. The believer's faith in the word of God will prepare the believer to enter God's gates with thanksgiving and praise.

This is the place where the prayer of the believer becomes fervent, understanding their righteousness through the word of God. This righteous believer is one who identifies themselves as an heir and joint heir with Christ, having believed and received the word of God that declares their covenant between God and themselves. The appropriate fear level found in the word of God will ensure the believer prepares themselves to come boldly (naked and broken) to the throne room of grace. This boldness is a result of receiving the word of God with understanding and allowing the Holy Spirit to voice this wisdom in one's lifestyle. This boldness enables the believer to speak when prompted by the Holy Spirit, and to keep quiet in the spirit when prompted by the Holy Spirit. Believers cannot deny this dispensation (church age) while withholding the only antidote for the forgiveness and penalty of sin with a silent tongue and an unrenewed mind.

Ambassador of Christ

All believers are charged to become ambassadors for Christ. The responsibilities and duties of an ambassador will require believers to spend quality and quantity time with God in prayer, praise, and worship. The duties as believers will require quality time spent searching the word of God for wisdom and understanding. The duties will also require believers to spend quality time in the presence of God in the cleft of the rock (Jesus).

This is the gate where believers meditate on the word of God day and night to result in establishing the righteousness pathway to follow. This is the gate believers begin exalting the word of God above all else, embracing the word of God to respectfully represent Christ. Duties and responsibilities as an ambassador also include understanding the purpose, plan, and intent of Jesus the Christ, whom the believer represents as an ambassador. Having spent quality time in the word of God, believers are fully aware that their thoughts and ways don't always represent the law of Christ.

As ambassadors, believers are charged to walk circumspectly. The word of God sets the standards for believers to conduct themselves in all facets of their lives. Jesus has delegated the authority to his body (church) to be the light of this world. Believers are to walk circumspectly (carefully, discreetly) so that others can see the God in them. This call to be ambassadors will challenge the believer to follow after the goodness of God. Walking carefully to be found in Christ as a child of God, born from on high, putting away the incorruptible seed of the flesh. This call to represent the God believers serve forces the believer to walk in love in the same manner Christ loved the believer. Believers understand that as ambassadors of Christ, the gift of God's grace is on display and desires a sweet-smelling savor.

This is the season when the ambassadors of Christ fight the good fight of faith to have no fellowship with the unfruitful works and reproving any doctrine of false teaching. This is the season ambassadors of Christ demonstrate their unstoppable strength, their unmovable faith to glorify God in and out of season. Believers acting as ambassadors for Christ purposely seek the lost souls for restoration to God. Believers representing Christ redeem the times in haste to tell the story that Jesus is a better way. Believers labor fervently in prayer and fellowship with those God has placed in their path. This is the phase when believers are pursuing God's heart (loving and valuing the same things God does) to live in a manner that glorifies God. Believers understand that much time has been wasted and recognize that the last hour is before the church. Believers as ambassadors work the work of the one that they represent with an endless zeal, while time permits. This is the mature level in God where the believer takes on the charge to be the light of the world, the salt of the earth preserving the Kingdom of God until Jesus returns.

This is the mature level of believers that understands their position as ministers of Christ and are anointed as stewards of the mysteries of God's plan for mankind through the Holy Spirit. The Water Gate is the place believers continue in prayer with thanksgiving through the fear of God. This is the season when God has opened doors to speak the mysteries of the gospel of Jesus Christ. Believers walk in the wisdom of God with meekness before mankind to represent a God that can't be seen with physical eyes. This is the phase of the metamorphosis believers represent Christ as faithful servants, fighting the good fight of faith, yet acting as fools for Christ's sake. This is a time and place where believers ignore the chatter of the ungodly, the spirit of the antichrist, and seek to please God with the excitement of a neophyte and the wisdom of Solomon.

This is the mature level in God where believers as ambassadors take hold of the gospel of Jesus Christ as the power of God to save souls. This is a mature level where believers exercise their faith through the word of God written on the tables of their hearts, knowing that God is with them. This is season believers are referred to as the "Redeemed of the Lord."

Have you entered the Water Gate? Do you meditate on the word of God daily? Has the word become a spiritual food source you can't live without? I recommend seeking God's will, plan, and future for your life through the word of God. The word of God is the power of God unto salvation. If believers are going to accept the effectual calling to become ambassadors of Christ, meditating in the word of God is vital to observe to do according to his will.

Spiritual Growth

The Water Gate will develop believers who have committed their love toward God through service for the expansion of the Kingdom of God. Believers move from redemption at the Sheep Gate, through service in the Fish Gate, repentance in the Old Gate, deliverance in the Valley Gate, to cleansing in the Dung Gate, empowered in the Fountain Gate for God's purpose to true holiness in the Water Gate.

A successful Water Gate will show forth the believer as one who continuously purifies their soul by obeying the truth of the word of God through the voice of the Holy Spirit unto an unfeigned love toward God and mankind. This is the place where the revealing of Christ through the word of God has provided wisdom that Jesus is imminent (close, near, at hand, approaching, impending); Jesus is transcending (his ways and thoughts are unparalleled); Jesus is intimate (resting in the heart of the believer), closely acquainted, familiar, faithful, special; Jesus is also intimidating (holy and fearful) and frightening.

It is the adult believers (those who have accepted the effectual calling of God) who are charged to evangelize and pray with anointing from on high. It is the spiritual adult believers who are charged to use the gift(s) and talent(s) from God to effectively use the word of God, the power in the name of Jesus, and the blood of Jesus for a hurting world. Having experienced these promises, the believer is charged to cleanse themselves from all filthiness of the flesh in the fear of God.

Adult Butterfly Ready for Spiritual Warfare: The Horse Gate

Butterflies are prey for birds, spiders, lizards, small mammals, and other insects. Their defense mechanism includes camouflage (blending into their surroundings) and coloration that warns predators of possible poisonous chemicals. These are physical defense weapons against predators of the butterfly aimed to stop the glory of God in its existence and in its splendor.

Liken unto the butterfly, believers have been equipped with spiritual weaponry to stand against a spiritual predator designed to kill, steal, and destroy the believer's good works and stop the advancement of the Kingdom of God. This is the phase of the metamorphosis when believers have become living sacrifices that walk in the flesh and may have to engage in physical battle to defend themselves. However, the change at the new birth (Sheep Gate) is spiritual, and the believer has a spiritual enemy. This enemy will use anything and anyone under his authority to exalt himself against the word of God. This is the same enemy in times past when the believer walked in the spirit of the god of this world as a child of disobedience. This is the same enemy that reigned in times past over those blinded by the god of this world. This enemy will use the people closest to you to bring about doubt in the believer's faith walk with God. This spiritual enemy brings fear, doubt, and deception to fight against the promises and blessing of God's word and the believer's call to be a member of the body of Christ, whom they represent on this earth.

The Horse Gate

This is the place where the god of this world and all his resources will attack every ounce of the believer to kill, steal, and destroy their good works. Spiritual warfare is war against everything God has promised in his word. The Horse Gate is related to spiritual warfare. The Horse Gate speaks to believers of war, as horses became the vehicle in battle. The Horse Gate has become a symbol of war, as the King of Kings and the Lord of Lords will return to judge and make war on a white horse.

Spiritual warfare will surely come as the believer

grows in faith through the word of God and begins appropriating the wisdom and understanding to further the Kingdom of God. This is the place where believers will experience spiritual conflict against the work and effort of every force that presents itself against the knowledge of God. The good fight of faith is not a fight against mankind in the physical capacity. There is the realization of the unseen realm that has spiritual effects that can be seen by physical attributes. It's likened unto the wind; mankind can see the effects of the wind but are unable to see the essence (unable to determine its character) of the wind.

It is very difficult to logically comprehend a threat from things that cannot be seen within mankind's physical senses. However, the word of God has warned believers there is a war going on in the spiritual realm against all believers. The word of God has also prepared the believer to win the war in advance through spiritual weaponry. This fight of faith is more than just a fight to maintain the believer's faith. The battles of faith and the victories will sustain the believer's love toward mankind aimed to relieve them of the yoke of this world. These spiritual battles will propel believers to follow after Christ, choosing him as preeminent in everything they do.

Spiritual metamorphosis is a spiritual ordeal and has nothing or very little to do with the physical realm outside of glorifying God as living sacrifices. From the beginning of this spiritual metamorphosis, the believer experiences an unexplainable presence that cannot be explained in layman's terms. The Sheep Gate experience alone goes beyond the physicality and intellect of mankind's ability to reason, beyond mankind's consciousness, beyond the things that exceed the human capacity to reason. Because this is a spiritual metamorphosis, there are spiritual temptations, spiritual confusion, spiritual discernment, and spiritual forces that will fight against the believer's faith in the word of God. These forces will attempt to deter the believer from presenting their body as a living sacrifice, to live holy unto God. One of the aims and the intent of the enemies of this world is to discredit Christ's ambassadors and agents.

The god of this world will show himself in many ways, from a red scary devil with pointy horns to a voice trying to get the believer to commit unspeakable acts that goes against the knowledge of God. The work of evil can look as mundane as spreading hurtful gossip about someone to hypocrisy in the body of Christ. The god of this word is crafty and is willing to wait for the believer to awake without their armor—unsober, unvigilant, carefree—to attack and cause a setback to the expansion of the Kingdom of God. There is a spiritual war going on between the god of this world and the body of Christ. The unseen force of evil wants to bring doubt and deception that God loves mankind, even in their fallen state, and desires to bring them into the Kingdom of God.

The Horse Gate Experience

The Horse Gate is a place where the believer no longer allows the fleshly desires to control their lives but waits on the Holy Spirit for direction and guidance. The Horse Gate is the place believers realize that the fight of faith has never been against flesh and blood, but a spiritual force of evil to derail the purpose and plan of God for mankind. These evil forces are designed to destroy any attempt to glorify God in this world as witnesses that God loves mankind even in their fallen state.

The good news is that Jesus has already defeated these forces and has given believers the authority and power over these forces. The believer's responsibility is to acknowledge that these evil forces exist. This is the mature level in Christ that believers trust that Jesus has paid the price for their sins and rely completely on the Holy Spirit to be a standard against the wiles of the enemy. This is the place and time that believers rely and depend on the counseling and help of the Holy Spirit to avoid the unseen enemy's traps.

This is the phase of the spiritual metamorphosis when the word of God becomes the believer's umpire (an authoritarian source to enforce rules). The wiles of the enemy and unseen forces will influence the believer's decision-making processes. The thoughts and imagination of the old man are yet alive in the believer's members and aim to dictate as much as the believer allows it to control. Even when mankind has good intentions, their actions and reactions can be indifferent when faced with opposition from unseen force(s). In this battle it is understood that the believer will serve the law of God in their renewed mind (Water Gate) as the flesh will fight to serve the law of the old man full of sin. The believer is forever putting on the new man and putting off the old man as the old man dies day by day. The regenerated spirit of the believer is renewed daily; however, the flesh will remain flesh until physical death occurs, separating the believer from the law of sin or until Jesus's return.

The union between God and the believer settles the issues of authority over the enemies of this world. The Spirit of God that dwells in the believer is upon the believer for spiritual conflict. The wisdom and understanding of the word of God voiced with confidence and righteousness will cause the enemies to flee. This is the phase of the metamorphosis when the believer speaks to the unseen forces with authority informing them of the blood of Jesus and the covenant they have with him. In the Horse Gate the believer reaches a mature level where they are recognized by the anointing and grace that they possess. Mankind can see the anointing and the faith of the Horse Gate believer and find comfort in their present. The Horse Gate believer abides under the shadow of the Almighty, as the Spirit of the God is always present to lift up a standard (barrier, hedge) against the enemies of this world. This standard presented by the Spirit of God will surely bring salvation unto believers and sustain the believer in any spiritual battle. The Spirit of God will stop the enemy and put them to flight or drive them away. This is the season the Horse Gate believers are aware of the spiritual battle found in the Water Gate experience. They are aware and settle in their hearts that they are heirs of salvation, that the presence of God is more than the world against them. This is the mature level of the Horse Gate believer remaining firm in their faith accomplished in the Water Gate. The Horse Gate believer is active in their relationship and communion with Christ in their faith walk.

A successful Fountain and Water Gate experience has spiritually equipped the believer with ammunition, with weaponry designed to stand against the spiritual enemy. The weapons obtained in the successful Fountain and Water Gate experiences enable the believer to rightly discern spiritual attacks dressed up in sheep clothing. These spiritual forces aim to stop the furthering of the Kingdom of God, to kill, steal, and destroy the promises and blessings of God that demonstrates God's presence and power on this earth. The Fountain and the Water Gates have brought the believer to a level of maturity in Christ that they have been formed by God, redeemed by God, and are a child of God. The Horse Gate believer is aware of their rights and privileges and the anointing to walk through the fire of the enemy in faith without staggering. The Horse Gate is the place where believers use the wisdom of God's word and their personal relationship to stand as one precious and honorable in God's sight. Believers in this phase stand against the unseen forces of evil; they are fearless because of who God is and His spirit that dwells with them.

The believer's life will be preserved by using the weapons of God's vast array of resources available for warfare against a spiritual fold. The Holy Spirit's attributes and presence in the believer's spirit will preserve them until they finish their course (God's plan for their lives). These weapons are not designed to be used against mankind in the physical realm. These weapons are designed for pulling down imaginations, bringing every doubt and evil perception into captivity. The Horse Gate is the place where sacrifice, patience, and obedience as ambassadors and agents of Christ are on display for a hurting world to witness the power of God.

The Sheep Gate experience arms the believer with weapons to fight off spiritual forces. These weapons have been at the disposal of the believer without the necessary training and instructions on how to use them effectively. The word of God, the name of Jesus, the blood of Jesus, prayer, praise, worship, and the words of the believer's testimonies are weapons against any spiritual fold. These spiritual weapons require the appropriate application in each realm to effectively cause victory over the enemy. The Holy Spirit is the master of these weapons and the use of them. He has the intel, and he is omnipotence (the source of all power), omnipresence (predominant), and omniscience (all-knowing, aware of the past, present, and future) regarding the enemy and his strategy to derail believers from glorifying God. The success of the Water Gate will provide not only the power of God unto salvation but will also acknowledge a constant instructor with refreshing ability to stay abreast of the enemy's strategy to stop, delay, or confuse the believer's mission.

Belt of Truth

One of the most important spiritual weapons is the Belt of Truth. As with the Sheep Gate, the Belt of Truth is Jesus the Christ. Jesus and the word of God is one in itself. A successful Water Gate and a continued effort seeking the knowledge of Jesus Christ equip the believers with spiritual discernment to recognize and fight against any fold. All spiritual blessings, benefits, protection, peace, joy, and many other liberties begin with knowing Jesus Christ as Lord and Savior. The Belt of Truth is Jesus the Christ, on which all the laws and prophets hang. This Belt of Truth is the gospel of Jesus the Christ and the power of God unto salvation. This Belt of Truth is anointed with the Holy Spirit, with power and authority over any enemies in this world. The indwelling Holy Spirit is more than enough to defeat the spiritual enemy and its tricks of deception. Soldiers of Christ should never go into battle without their Belt of Truth that holds spiritual ammunition, power, weapons, and everything the believer (soldier of God) will need to win the battle in advance. This is the phase when believers understand they are more than conquerors having received the spoils of the victory over death, hell, and the grave.

The Belt of Truth holds ammunition for spiritual warfare. This Belt of Truth has ammo pouches that store testimonies developed in the Valley Gate that Jesus is a redeemer. The word of God rooted and grounded in the believer is used by the Holy Spirit as the believer's umpire. This umpire will allow the believer to be steadfast (unmovable) against opposition. The Holy Spirit has proven with tangible and intangible evidence that the gospel of Jesus Christ is real and powerful. These truths are demonstrated through the fruit and character of the Holy Spirit as believers walk in the Spirit of God displaying honesty, integrity, truthfulness, and sincerity.

I'm reminded of the story in the Old Testament where Elijah the prophet of God in Israel was sought after by an enemy. The enemy came with horses and chariots by night to a place called Dothan. Elijah awoke to a host of horses and chariots to take him captive alone with one of Elijah's young servants. The servant asked Elijah, "How shall we do?" Modern-day vernacular would be something like, "What shall we do? We are doomed." The prophet of God, Elijah, prayed to the Almighty God to open the spiritual eyes of the young lad so that he could see in the spiritual realm what could not be seen in nature. God opened the young lad's eyes, and he saw the mountain was full of spiritual horses and chariots of fire around Elijah and himself. One of the first things I noticed was that Elijah, the prophet of God, had already discerned

God's providential intervention. God's forces for his protection were already in formation ahead of the enemy's attack. Elijah had on the whole armor of God.

The Belt of Truth (apparatus) is the foundation of a soldier's gear and holds and carries spiritual ammunition (indwelling Spirit of God) to sustain the fight of faith until the believer finishes their course or until Jesus returns for His church.

Breastplate of Righteousness

Another weapon God has given believers is the Breastplate of Righteousness. The Breastplate of Righteousness is the truth of God's word realized, believed, and accepted by faith. Believers walking in the Spirit of God in obedience and agreement with God produce daily righteousness. This obedience and daily righteousness become the believer's spiritual Breastplate of Righteousness. This truth realized is the believer's faith in Jesus the Christ that "got up" from the grave for the believer's justification. This truth realized is knowing that nothing can separate the believer from the love of God. This truth realized leads the believer to holiness and the fear of God for change. This truth realized identifies the believer as the likeness of God's character.

The Breastplate of Righteousness is a constant reminder to repent daily to ensure "right standing" with God. This is the place and season the believer continues to allow the Water Gate experience to cleanse and purify their soul. This is the season the believer understands the fullness of the atoning work on the cross as it pertains to righteousness. The believer's faith and relationship established in the Valley Gate that recognize Jesus as their "Lord of Righteousness" will secure the Breastplate of Righteousness with the Belt of Truth.

This is the mature phase of the metamorphosis when the believer is prone to be sober, and vigilant is their priority in understanding the threat level of their spiritual battle. The Breastplate of Righteousness is not earned through good behavior, but in knowing the truth that Jesus Christ made the believer's righteousness with God through His work on the cross. The believer understands that the "truth realized," that Jesus the Christ is the propitiation of the sin for mankind, has made the believer righteous.

This is the mature phase of the spiritual metamorphosis when the believer is walking in obedience and agreement to the word of God (righteousness). The Horse Gate believer is aware of the enemy's plot and has consciously ensured that the Breastplate of Righteousness and the Belt of Truth are securely aligned and attached to one another. The Belt of Truth coupled with the believer's testimonies of God's grace is more than enough firepower to defeat any spiritual enemy.

This Breastplate of Righteousness and other attachments of the armor of God are provided at the point the believer repents and accepts Jesus Christ as their Lord and Savior. It is the Belt of Truth (Jesus Himself) that keeps the Breastplate of Righteousness (truth realized that the believer is the righteousness of God) from moving away from its purpose to come boldly to the throne room of the Grace of God. It is the believer's position to keep the Belt of Truth and the Breastplate of Righteousness securely fastened to one another.

Gospel of Peace

The Gospel of Peace is the good news that Jesus Christ the long-awaited Messiah has come, and the penalty of sin has been paid in full. This good news (love of God) is available to whomsoever will believe. This good news (God's grace) will fit the believer with the Gospel of Peace, allowing the believer to receive the good news with assurance.

The Gospel of Peace is the believer's position with Christ, the believer's union with Christ, the believer's love for Christ. The believer's position with Christ is a time and season the believer understands that they have received the righteousness of Christ and are blameless in God's sight, yet their condition as living sacrifices is not equally yoked. The believer's legal status having been declared not guilty of acts of sin has nothing to do with the believer's condition in the world. The Dung Gate experience (dying to self) will amplify the flesh weakness, as there is not a good thing in the flesh. This position in Christ labels the believers as new creations in Christ Jesus. The East Gate believer is patiently awaiting the consummation of God's promise to be in the presence of Christ for eternity. The Inspection Gate experience will manifest the hope of the believer's salvation where the believer's condition will be a carbon copy of their legal position in Christ. The Inspection Gate will confirm believers are complete in Christ, who is the head of all principalities and power.

The believer's union with Christ identifies the believer has risen with Christ and their life is hidden with Christ in God. The believer is identified with God, accepted in the beloved as a new creature, and the nature of the believer is new in God's sight. The Apostle Paul speaks to the union with Christ as being found in him, not having his own righteousness, but through faith to receive the righteousness which is of God by faith. The union with Christ is apprehending Christ that apprehended him. The union with Christ provides insight into the heart of God and the power associated with the resurrection of Jesus Christ. The union with Christ has to do with the fellowship of Jesus's suffering, yet comfort, unto the death of the cross. "And the life I now live in the flesh I live by faith in the Son of God, who loved me and gave himself for me."

The East Gate believer is aware that love is from God, and nothing can separate the believer from the love of Christ. The East Gate believer's love for Christ is discovered by their obedience to God's word. This demonstration of the love of God through obedience is one to whose soul God will reveal himself.

The Gospel of Peace is the precious promise of God that speaks to being sealed by the Holy Spirit, filled with the Holy Spirit, covered by the blood of Jesus, that all things work out for the good to them that love God and are called according to his purpose.

This is the place where the believer maintains their weaponry, ensuring the Belt of Truth (Jesus the Christ) and the Breastplate of Righteousness (truth realized) are aligned and attached securely to each other. The Gospel of Peace (believer's position in the Kingdom) will allow the believer to stand their ground in the face of the wiles of the enemy to derail God's plan for their life. The Horse Gate believer is fitted with designer shoes, or boots (rooted and built up in Christ) of peace, to keep the believer moving forward in the things of

God to take the gospel of Jesus Christ to others. These designer shoes of the Gospel of Peace maintain the believer's footing (established in the faith, truth realized) to share their faith with others, to glorify God, to honor God and provide a narrative of praise to whosoever's heart God has pricked to hear the truth. There is a peace in knowing the truth about who you are and whose you are. A peace that surpasses all logic and understanding. Jesus provides a peace that the believer cannot earn; it cannot be purchased and cannot be obtained through the world and its systems.

I'm reminded of the movie titled *Overcomer* where Hannah tells her track coach, "Ask me who I am." The coach entertains Hannah and asks her, "Who are you?" Hannah replies with confidence in her position in Christ (Gospel of Peace) and brings about a peace to all ears and minds under her voice.

Hannah replies, "I'm created by God. He designed me, so I'm not a mistake; His Son died for me, just so I can be forgiven; He picked me to be His own, so I'm chosen; He redeemed me so I'm wanted; He showed me grace, just so I can be saved. He has a future for me because He loves me. So, I don't wonder anymore. I'm a child of God."

The believer's position in Christ is not based on the believer's own righteousness, natural abilities, or worthiness. The believer's Gospel of Peace is the revelation knowledge, wisdom, and understanding of Jesus's work on the cross and his acceptance of God the Father.

Shield of Faith

The Shield of Faith is the first barrier against the enemy's attack to impede the believer's spiritual growth. The believer's faith and experience of God's faithfulness are sufficient to shield the believer from the wiles of the enemy. This is the place where the believer is to hold on to their faith, to choose faith regardless of the circumstances or expected outcome. This Shield of Faith is developed in the Valley Gate with evidence of God's grace, not blind belief. The Shield of Faith is the believer's protective barrier not only to fight off the enemy, but to push back to gain ground to share the gospel of Jesus Christ.

This is the phase in the believer's life when they recognize that Jesus is their Shield of Faith (word of God). It is Jesus that covers the believer from the top of his head to the bottom of his feet (clothed in righteousness). This is the season when the Horse Gate believer abides in Christ in the spiritual realm and the enemy can only see Jesus, the Lord of Lords, King of Kings. This is the place where faith in Christ's position seated at the right hand of God provides a peace and confidence in times of trouble. This is the phase of the spiritual metamorphosis when the believer "lifts up" the Shield of Faith (Jesus) for the restoration of mankind to God and finds refuge in that faith. The truth of God's promises and the believer's faith developed through the transformation become a shield for deliverance, a shield for grace toward others, and a shield from the arrows of deception from the enemy. This is the season the Horse Gate believer's faith in God's word becomes the believer's buckler (portable shield) in spiritual warfare. Jesus has provided believers the gift of faith to stand through the knowledge of Him and God the Father.

I'm reminded of the story of Jesus being led by the Holy Spirit into the wilderness to be tempted of the devil. At Jesus's weakest moment in the flesh, He held up the Shield of Faith and declared the word of God (logos), stating, "It is written." The Shield of Faith will settle the believer's countenance with confidence and boldness.

Helmet of Salvation and Sword of the Spirit

The helmet is the last item the soldier puts on. This helmet is a defensive tool used against the wiles of the enemy. The Helmet of Salvation is better understood as the hope of the believer's salvation. This is the kind of hope (earnest hope) that fills the gap between prayer for deliverance and the manifestation of those prayers. The hope of the believer's salvation requires the believer to trust and rely on what cannot be seen. This is where the Holy Spirit takes hold of the believer's flesh through obedience and empowers and propels the believer through their weaknesses. This hope is dependent on the Holy Spirit to see through the intent and the motives of the enemy. This is the place where the Holy Spirit becomes the believer's "intel" to discern the plan and strategies of the enemy before impact. This Helmet of Salvation (hope of salvation) is critical to the warfare that is set up against all believers.

The Sword of the Spirit (word of God) keeps the believer in peace knowing that Jesus the Christ has already given the believer the victory through his work on the cross. The Horse Gate is a time and season when believers need not fight this fight of spiritual warfare in their own strength; the victory belongs to God. The enemy has already been defeated; it's a fixed fight and the believer wins.

The word of God (Sword of the Spirit) reminds believers that God has given them authority and power over all the power of the enemy. The Horse Gate believers are aware of this threat and act accordingly by putting on the whole armor of God.

Spiritual Growth

The believer has moved from the Water Gate, building standards and spiritual muscles to finish their course. The Horse Gate is the phase of the metamorphosis when believers will experience the attack from the god of this world amplified. The god of this world has worked hard to keep mankind from entering the Sheep Gate, worked hard against the believer to evangelize the gospel of Jesus Christ, worked hard to keep the believer from obeying the word of God, worked hard to kill, steal, and destroy the believer's faith and relationship experienced in the Valley Gate, worked hard to maintain the depravity and weakness in the believer in the Dung Gate, worked hard to confuse the believer regarding the anointing of God on the believer's life to accomplish God's purpose in the Fountain Gate, worked hard to deny the revealing of Jesus Christ, and now the enemy of this world desires to control the believer and derail the purpose and plan of God in the Horse Gate. The battle of these spiritual forces is in the mind of the believer and requires faith (lifestyle acting on God's word) to prevail against the god of this world. The faith walk is vital to defeat the enemy and requires voiced testimonies from believer's experiences in each gate of their spiritual metamorphosis. These testimonies will ward off the enemy, as the voice of faith through praising God causes his intervention and faithfulness to his word. The trying of one's faith through the Valley Gate and the gift of God receiving Christ as Lord will enable believers to submit themselves to God, resisting the enemy and ensuring his departure.

The Horse Gate believer moves from confidence and faith in Jesus Christ to be seated with Him in heavenly places. This is the season the Horse Gate believer rests in Jesus Christ with a childlike faith. This is the mature phase of the spiritual metamorphosis when the wisdom of God (gospel of Jesus Christ) is at work in the believer for mankind to witness the power of God through the fear of God. The Horse Gate believer's understanding is that God's grace is sufficient in any circumstance. This is the place where the Horse Gate believer has no confidence in their own strength but in the strength of God's might. The Horse Gate believer begins to lay down their burdens by the riverside, trusting in God's grace (enabler) to enjoy a sabbath rest. This is the time and season the believer downloads God's grace received in the Water Gate that God will preserve their life, that God will strengthen them with his right hand of righteousness. This is the season the believer recognizes that God is their strength, that God is their fortress, and in Him alone they have life and the life they live is by faith in

Jesus Christ. This is the phase of the spiritual metamorphosis that the Horse Gate believer has gained patience (steadfastness), downloaded God's strength, and strengthened their faith with confidence to ensure a just reward. This is the phase of the metamorphosis when the Horse Gate believer rests in the Gospel of Peace (quiet place, resting in the word of God).

The revealing of Christ through the word of God has provided wisdom that Jesus is imminent, transcending, intimate, and intimidating. The Horse Gate believer receives the promises of God with unmovable faith that God is their shield and their reward. Have you experienced unseen forces fighting against your walk with Christ? Do you find yourselves constantly fighting to maintain your spiritual relationship with Christ? I recommend believers awake each morning combat-ready to walk the good fight of faith with the whole armor of God tightly fitted.

The believer's love for God and their reverential fear of God will cause victory in advance having known the end state and the spiritual value gained in the Water Gate (wisdom and knowledge of their covenant with Christ). God wants believers to understand that he has already won the battles and the war against anything that comes against His plan to reconcile mankind to Himself. God wants His children to delight in knowing that He will never leave them nor forsake them.

The essence of love for mankind found in the Fish Gate, the constant presence of love found in the Valley Gate, the fruit of love displayed in the lives of the believers experienced in the Dung Gate, the overshadowing and fullness of love emerged in the Holy Spirit at the Fountain Gate, and the love of God from the heart of God are more than enough to be identified with Christ. Believers are to keep in mind that Jesus is the avenger and deliverer of the body of Christ. It is through the power of the Holy Spirit that injustice against the body of Christ, the enemy, is destroyed.

The Horse Gate reminds believers that Jesus has won the war of the cross, the grave, and death, providing believers the freedom to live for Christ. The Horse Gate reminds believers of Jesus's coming on a white horse to battle with the enemy of this world. The Horse Gate reminds believers that they are more than conquerors in battle. Jesus has conquered death, hell, and the grave. Believers have received the spoils of Jesus's victory, receiving all that Jesus accomplished in battle without laboring. The Horse Gate is a place and time when the believer's purpose and plan for their lives is closer than ever before. This is the place where signs and wonders are following believers as they obey the voice of the Holy Spirit. The Horse Gate is the place where life and death are in the power of the believer's spoken word (rhema). God's word has come alive in them! The believer's ability to hear and obey the indwelling Holy Spirit will clearly identify things pertaining to God.

Making Disciples of Jesus Christ: The East Gate

The adult butterfly drinks nectar from its primary food source for reproduction purposes. Nectar is an organic source filled with the proteins, salt, acids, and essential oils necessary for life. The adult butterfly gets its energy from the food source to reproduce and lay eggs for future existence.

Likewise, the East Gate believer meditates on the word of God (nectar), the incorruptible seed, to reproduce the likeness of God and the image of Jesus Christ. The East Gate believer has accepted the effectual calling to preach the gospel, to feed God's lamb and to feed God's sheep. This is a season when believers are allowing their light to shine with grace and truth, providing others the strength to come out of the closet of fear, to come out of the closet of self-righteousness, to come out of the closet of despair. This is a time when believers are actively engaged in God's business reaping dividends in the Kingdom of God from knowledge learned from phase to phase. This is the season the believer is bold as a lion; nothing moves them from obeying God's plan and promises using God's grace as an enabler to accomplish God's mission. This is the season believers receive the ministry appointed unto them to testify of the gospel and the grace of God.

This is a maturity level in the complete metamorphosis where the East Gate believer returns to the Fish Gate experience, evangelizing and making full proof of the gospel of Christ and the grace of God. This is a time when believers are afflicted in the affliction of others. This is the place where East Gate believers comfort others as they have been comforted by God. This is the gate where believers are not moved by the politics and the changing culture that worship the creature more than the creator. This is the place where East Gate believers are acting as the salt of the earth to preserve the faith and the power of God until the Son of God returns for His church. The East Gate believers at this phase of the spiritual metamorphosis are defending the gospel, not in pretense but in truth. This is the season the East Gate believer is preaching Jesus loves mankind and has made a way of escape from their sins and the punishment of sin without merit.

The East Gate

The East Gate is one of two gates that one can use to gain access to the City of Jerusalem from the east. Jewish tradition believes that the Shekinah (divine presence of God) has appeared through the East Gate. This is the gate the word of God declares that Jesus the Christ (Anointed One) will use to enter Jerusalem on his second coming.

The East Gate reminds believers of the return of Jesus Christ. Jesus said, "If I go and prepare a place for you, I will come again and receive you unto myself; that where I am, there ye may be also." Prophecy declares as "lightning come out of the east, and shines unto the west, so shall the coming of the Son of Man be." The East Gate reminds believers of their hope of complete salvation at Jesus's appearance to spend eternity with Christ.

This is a time and season when believers have taken advantage of the many opportunities to be a blessing (position of God's provisions) in someone else's life. The East Gate is a place and time that believers are aware of and are committed to the gifts, talents, and God's anointing to express the love of God as living sacrifices. The East Gate is a place where the believer is using their gifts and talents to endure the influence of today's culture and to go beyond their own will to do the will of God. The East Gate believer is rejoicing in giving and being used by God to further the Kingdom of God. God's grace has propelled the East Gate believer to make known the gospel of Jesus Christ to mankind. These promises of influence as God's people are equipped with an anointing from God to reach those who are lost. The East Gate believer is fully persuaded they have been justified, able to stand before God blameless. This is the place where East Gate believers are turning the key to spiritual maturity to activate their reasonable service to God. The believer now tells the story that Jesus Christ loves mankind and has made a way of escape from this dark world.

This is the mature phase of the metamorphosis when East Gate believers are taking the yoke of God and Jesus Christ, whom He sent to find rest for their souls. This is the phase of the metamorphosis when East Gate believers are holding on to their Valley Gate experience knowing God will work out all things for the good, knowing that God is all knowing and forever present in a time of help. This is the gate where East Gate believers are setting the standard by demonstrating godly values and concerns for the well-being of others. This is the phase when the East Gate believers are searching for accessories fitting for the promise to be clothed in righteousness, dressing for the occasion with confidence and love at Jesus's appearance.

This is the phase of the metamorphosis when the East Gate believers are taking hold of their effectual calling with the aim and purpose to magnify Christ, whether as living sacrifices or their spiritual legacy (long-lasting impact). This is the season East Gate believers are standing as witnesses and partakers of Christ's suffering. This is the place where East Gate believers are fulfilling their calling unto eternal glory (perfect, establish, strengthen, and settle) in Christ Jesus. This the season East Gate believers are experiencing a spiritual phenomenon (unable to be observed through mankind's senses) having a desire to be with Christ, as this world has nothing to offer. This is the season East Gate believers are standing with their conversation seasoned with salt (becoming the gospel of Christ) subject only to the things of God (pure heart) and living to please God (righteous vessel). The East Gate is a mature spiritual level where the believer's narrative is of a sound speech, no condemnation toward mankind, only showing themselves a pattern of good works.

This is the place where the believer experiences the fullness of eternal life learned through the knowledge of God and Jesus Christ, whom He sent. The East Gate believer has the propensity to favor the thoughts of their constant reminder (Holy Spirit) to think on things that are true, honest, pure, lovely, and good report. The East Gate believer is persistently purifying their soul fitting to an unfeigned love with a pure heart for the lost in this world. This is a mature spiritual level where believers are laboring to reach those unsure regarding their salvation (lamb), laboring to reach the lost sheep who are afraid to give up the things of this world, laboring to remain steadfast in the gospel of Jesus Christ as stewards of God's word to demonstrate God's presence in this world. This is the metamorphosis phase when believers are spiritual adults ready for reproducing the image of Christ. This is the phase East Gate believers are standing in the gap for all those that God has placed in their midst in one spirit with the same mind striving for the faith of the gospel. This is a time when believers accept the challenge to act as the salt of the earth, ministers of Christ, ambassadors of Christ, children of the Most High God, preserving the earth until Jesus's appearance. The East Gate is where believers are working and laboring with a good conscience serving God in patience as a "hallmark" regarding their relationship with Christ. The East Gate is where believers have perfected the Dung Gate experience in putting away childish things, all bitterness, wrath, and anger, walking in the Spirit of God while denying self. This is the season believers are preparing themselves for Jesus's appearance as a glorious church unrebukable and without the smut of a fallen culture.

This is the phase of the complete metamorphosis when believers are steadfast in the work of God, pushing the limits continually to accomplish the will of God by preaching the gospel of Jesus Christ. When Jesus return for His church, He will find the East Gate believers laboring in love the ministry of reconciliation. This is the season East Gate believers are laboring faithfully and loyally to the work of God through the Holy Spirit.

The East Gate Experience

This is the phase of the metamorphosis that believers have looked back over their lives and acknowledged where God has brought them from.

This is the phase when believers are not only acknowledging where God has brought them from, but giving God praise for life eternal (Grace to receive the truth). The East Gate is a time of preparation for Jesus's appearance for His church and what He will find the believers doing when He comes. This gate will propel the believer to be steadfast in their profession of faith and examine themselves in preparation for Jesus's appearance prior to his second coming.

The East Gate, unlike the Sheep Gate, is more than the inception of the believer as sons and daughters of God but has subjugated the believer under the gift of faith in their "hope of glory" regarding Jesus's appearance for His church. The East Gate will propel the believer to not only remain steadfast in their profession of faith (act of declaration of who God is) but will reveal their possession of faith (act of engrafted word of God). The East Gate is a time and place where believers are taking inventory of the spoils (peace, joy, well-being, etc.) taken in spiritual battles that they didn't have to fight. The East Gate is where the believer will stand in full assurance of their end state in preparation at Jesus's appearance for His church. This is a time and place where believers are setting the stage for Jesus's appearance. The believer must ensure that their heart is pure and prepared to stand before the King of Kings and Lord of Lords.

The East Gate is the gate where the believer recognizes that the joy and peace of their salvation has empowered and propelled them to tell the story that God loves mankind. The East Gate is a place where believers consider their ways regarding their relationship with Christ, their spiritual growth, and their ability to reproduce the likeness of Christ. This is the gate where believers are accounting for God's investment in their lives, accounting for the people

God places in their care, accounting for the returns on God's gifts, talents, power, and promises to edify the Kingdom of God. This is the season that the East Gate believer is reviewing all that God has made them stewards over to ensure spiritual dividends. This is the place where the believer rejoices in their journey in full confidence that the complete metamorphosis has prepared them to entertain and rejoice at Jesus's appearance. This is the gate where believers are rejoicing at His appearance, having taken on the ministry of reconciliation furthering the Kingdom of God through the work of the Holy Spirit. The East Gate is the place where the believer understands when the Son of Man shall come in His glory that they will be with Him for eternity.

This is a season when believers are using God's grace to restore their strength, making room for God's provision to finish their course. This restoration empowers the East Gate believer to raise their spiritual credit score through faithfulness toward God, through their commitment to serve God to further the Kingdom of God, through their committed service to the purpose and plan of God for their lives. This restoration power enables East Gate believers to call on the name of Jesus for deliverance with covenant rights. The East Gate covenant right includes the Water Gate experience (God writing his laws on their heart), the Sheep Gate experience (reconciled to God, sanctified, made holy), the Valley Gate experience (God revealing himself), and the East Gate experience (empowered and equipped to produce the likeness of Christ). The East Gate believers have personally secured the new covenant promises by relying, trusting, and obeying God's commandments. The New Testament covenant promises of a new heart and new spirit that has caused the East Gate believer to walk in God's statutes unconsciously. This new covenant has caused the East Gate believer to be sanctified (free from the power and penalty of sin), holy unto God as a living sacrifice, and the character of the East Gate believer emulates that of the Spirit of God. This new covenant inheritance is evidence of the believer's new spirit having been reconciled to God through Christ Jesus. The East Gate believers are peculiar people (remarkable), having tapped into God's grace to finish their course. This new covenant has provided access unto God, no more strangers and foreigners, but fellow citizens in the household of God. The East Gate believer lives in a state of harmony with God as the first man, Adam, in the garden of Eden.

This is a time and place where believers are experiencing the awesome grace of God that cannot be told in its fullness. This is the mature phase of the metamorphosis when adult believers are anticipating the fullness of life eternal (relationship with the true God and Jesus, whom He sent) and the end of their faith and salvation for their souls. The East Gate is a place where believers accept the gift of salvation to hear and receive the things of God without the enemy's interference. This is the season East Gate believers are preaching the gospel of Jesus Christ without ceasing, reproving, and rebuking with the love of God anything that goes against the word of God. This is the phase of the metamorphosis when East Gate believers are experiencing a life of adventure awaiting what God will do next in their lives. This is the season that East Gate believers are totally dependent on God's promises for life's daily endeavors. The power of the indwelling Holy Spirit is more prominent in the believer's life now more than ever before.

The East Gate will allow believers to entertain and return to their Fish Gate experience (evangelizing). This is a place and season when believers are evangelizing (profession of faith) the word of God in preparation of Jesus's appearance. This is the mature phase of the metamorphosis when believers' actions are aligned to their profession and possession of their faith. The East Gate is where believers' steadfastness in the gospel of Jesus Christ is expressed for others to witness. It is a season when believers are separating themselves from the darkness of this world and the modern-day trends of ungodliness. This is the gate where believers are keeping their doorstep prepared for the welcoming of Jesus Christ. This the gate where the believer has purchased oil (obeying God's commandments as a choice) for their lamps in preparation for Jesus's arrival. This is a place where the believer's hope of salvation is sure, and the promise of eternal life (experiencing God and Jesus, whom He sent) is at hand. This is the season when believers continue to fight the good fight of faith, laying hold on eternal life and preserving the time until Jesus's appearance for His church. This is the season believers are taking responsibility for their work regarding the expansion of the Kingdom of God, telling the story that Jesus is Lord. This is the season believers are experiencing the forever Dung Gate (dying to self), separating themselves (sanctifying) from the old man's nature. The East Gate is the place where believers are keeping the articles of the upper room (bread of lives and the blood of Jesus) of their lives active in order to free themselves from the trends and fashions of this world, ready to rejoice at His appearance. This is the time the East Gate believers are making preparation for Jesus's appearance for His church, whose conscience has been purged from dead works.

This is the phase of the transformation believers

have no confidence in the flesh, sold out for God in the Spirit. The East Gate is the place believers are seeking and demonstrating the love of God (obedience) as witnesses of His church. This is the phase of the complete metamorphosis when believers accept and receive the truth that Jesus is the landlord and the keeper of their faith and love toward mankind.

Entering God's Rest

The East Gate is the place where believers have entered into God's rest. The East Gate is the mature believer that has moved from a Sabbath rest (practicing for eternity in God's presence) to dwelling and settling in Christ Jesus who is their rest (life eternal). The East Gate believer is patiently awaiting the consummation (make perfect, complete) of God's promise to be in the presence of Christ for eternity. This is the place where East Gate believers free themselves from the chaos of the completed Olivet Discourse (sign of Jesus's appearance) and remain steadfast to finish their course set before them. This is the adulthood phase of the spiritual metamorphosis when the believer's possession of faith aligns itself with their profession of faith, trusting and relying on God's word found in the Water Gate. God's rest has been sanctified (declared holy), blessed (positioned to receive God's provisions), and made holy (set apart for God's purpose) to East Gate believers. This is the season East Gate believers know that it was God and God alone who has kept them in His bosom (covering, embracing) and sustained them to this season of rest.

This is the phase of the spiritual metamorphosis believers rest in the whole armor of God. This is the season the East Gate believers stand in the power of their salvation (Belt of Truth) being found in Christ as the blood of Jesus has redeemed them and made a way of escape from themselves. The East Gate is the place believers are walking in the Spirit of God in obedience and agreement with God, producing righteousness and liberty as they repent daily. This is the season the believer continues to allow the Water Gate experience to cleanse and purify their soul (Breastplate of Righteousness). The East Gate is where believers experience the omnipresent God (always and everywhere you are). This omnipresence causes a healthy fear of Him, which causes a positive change in the believer. This is the season when believers are connecting Jesus and His work on the cross (Golgotha) together as a lifeline to the finishing of their faith. This level of believer receives Jesus Christ as the Son of God and the propitiation for their sins and builds their life on this cornerstone. The East Gate mature believer's hope (John 3:16) is engrafted in their heart, soul, and mind. This is the phase when believers are searching for the scriptures and waiting soberly and are watchful for His return. This is the place where the East Gate believer's spiritual position in Christ, their union and love for Christ, causes rest that only God can give (Gospel of Peace). This is the gate where the power of the "hope of salvation" is realized as the East Gate believer trusts and replies on their Water Gate experience (Helmet of Salvation). This is the season the East Gate believers acknowledge God's spiritual battle uniform (full armor of God) and make way to ensure it aligns with God's righteousness.

This is the season the East Gate believer rests in full assurance that their name is written in the "Who's Who" book of life (Lamb's book). The East Gate believer is fully persuaded that nothing can separated them from the love of God and death has no sting, therefore rest in Jesus is inevitable (bound to happen). The East Gate believer is considered a seasoned believer, identified by their commitment to keep the commandments of the word of God without compromising while living in a forever changing culture. The mindset of the East Gate believer is that of one who has remained blameless, without spots (worldly truth) and blemishes of this world, but in peace in Christ Jesus. This is the phase East Gate believers are not searching the highways and byways to smell the roses, but seeking those who are lost to tell the story of reconciliation to God, to tell the story that the appearance of Jesus Christ is near, and judgment is inevitable. This is the phase of spiritual adulthood where the East Gate believer is expressing the character of one who is sober, grave (serious), temperate, sound in their faith, full of charity and patience. This is the metamorphosis phase when adult believers are demonstrating the presence of God through a pattern and protocol of good works adorning the doctrine of God in sincerity. This is the gate where believers show themselves strong in the Lord and His might in the presence of others as true witnesses "as the amen of the word of God." This is the phase of the complete metamorphosis when East Gate believers are no longer playing small, hiding the power of the gift of faith from the world. This is the season of a mature believer that is using their gifts to preserve the earth as witnesses (faithful service) teaching and preaching the gospel of Jesus Christ to all whom God has placed in their midst. This is the phase of the metamorphosis when East Gate believers are far removed from the general calling of God's grace to the effectual calling to be committed to God's purpose and plan for their lives. This is the gate where believers are fulfilling the duties and responsibilities as "watchmen" over God's sheep and lambs, sharing the wisdom of God with certainty. This is the resting phase of the metamorphosis, when believers are holding their face to the windows of their lives constantly looking for the glorious appearing of Jesus the Christ. This is the season the believer does not concern themselves regarding the signs of the coming of Christ but looks upward anticipating His return. This is the season the East Gate believer identifies that the Valley (captivity designed by God), Dung (dying to self), and Horse Gate (spiritual warfare) experiences are found in praise and honor and glory at Jesus's appearing.

The East Gate believer is ready to receive the end of their faith with joy, setting their heart to default to the light in the inner man. This is the season East Gate believers quench not the grace of God to keep the hearts of the lost safe and comfortable but teach and preach the word of God in and out of season. This is the phase and season when the outward expression of the believer's love for God and God's love toward them is manifested to glorify God. The East Gate allows the believer to rest in a state of joy, awaiting the priceless promise of the hope of Jesus's appearance. This is the adult metamorphosis phase when the believer is standing in the judgment of God's word as "joint heirs with Christ" and benefactors of God's grace and mercy. The East Gate believer rests in a state of peace that surpasses all understanding that only

Christ can give, knowing that they will not suffer the second death. This is the season when the East Gate believers are enjoying a daily fellowship with Christ, sitting at the table of love each morning with Christ. The East Gate believer now has no agenda but to await God's direction through the power of the Holy Spirit.

The East Gate is a place where true believers return to the origin of God's plan for mankind (returning to the garden of life with perfect harmony) in a spiritual setting free from the curse of the law through the blood of Jesus Christ. The East Gate believer has come to their Rubicon (a point of no return), a place of "sold out" in full confidence that when Christ appears, they will receive their crown of righteousness. This is the season East Gate believers understand that the amazing power of the Son of Man has made them free from the bondage and the cares of this world. This is the place where East Gate believers separates themselves from a culture designed to dishonor God. This is a season when mature believers rest and rejoice in knowing that God promised that they would be kept from the hour of temptation.

Discerning the Times

This is the time when believers hold fast to their faith in the face of uncertainty. A time when believers accept the failure of their culture, as it tends to be diametrically opposed to the gospel of Jesus Christ. This is a time believers tighten the screws of God's righteousness received by faith and begin living sensibly and godly according to the word of God received and understood in the Water Gate.

This is the time believers recognize and discern the signs of Christ coming and sound the alarm warning believers to stand fast and hold on to their professions of faith. This is the gate where believers stay awake, sober, vigilant, praying and watching diligently for Jesus's return, shaking hands, and forgiving every remembered conflict of unrighteousness toward others.

This is a time when believers lift their Shield of Faith against the false teachers and prophets in this world. This is the time believers will speak against those in places of influence in this culture (scoffers) that laugh at the truth of God's word. This is the season believers will draw their Sword of the Spirit, cutting through false accusations of those who present themselves as antichrists. This is the gate where believers will stand against anything that comes against the knowledge of God (people that are lovers of themselves, lovers of money; people that are boastful; people that are proud, abusive, and many other characteristics of ungodliness). This is a time when true believers (those who worship God in spirit and truth) will separate themselves from those who have a form of godliness discerning the times. The East Gate is the place where believers are not shaken in their mind or troubled regarding the signs of Jesus's return. A time when believers are rooted and ground in the word of God and not easily deceived, never falling away from the truth, knowing that God is still on the throne and showing Himself to be God.

This is the mature level where the East Gate believers are redeeming the times to finish the plan of God for their lives willingly and effortless with joy demonstrating the power of life eternal. This is the mature level of the metamorphosis where believers are becoming empty vessels sharing the mystery of the Gospel of Jesus Christ with boldness speaking the word of God without fear.

The East Gate will allow believers to entertain their experience at the Fish Gate (service). A place where believers evangelize (profession of faith) the word of God. This is a time when believers' actions are aligned to their profession of faith. A place where believers are living by faith, not by sight; a place where believers are willing to wait on God for wisdom before moving.

The East Gate is a place where believers' steadfastness is expressed for others to witness. The Valley Gate experience has shepherded the believer to a lifestyle of declaring publicly their love for God. This public declaration led to sharing their testimonies as an outward expression of their relationship with God. This is the season when believers confess the bookends of life (Sheep Gate to the East Gate) to serve and mark the beginning and ending of their faith that surpasses all understanding, knowledge, and wisdom. The East Gate is the place where believers have finished their course, now awaiting Jesus's appearance. These bookends of life provide a sense of closure to the spiritual metamorphosis from inception at the Sheep Gate to the gathering of the soldiers of God (Church) in the Inspection Gate (at His appearance).

This is a time when believers acknowledge the prophecy of the end times and the signs leading to Christ's return. This is the gate where believers are preparing to avoid the troubling times before Jesus's unannounced return.

Spiritual Growth

This is the season when the East Gate believer is deployable to the call of God under the direction of the Holy Spirit without hesitation. The believer's course (race) set before them is clear, with spiritual blessings and provisions that only God can provide. The East Gate is a mature level of the metamorphosis where believers are walking in the Spirit of God, being led by the Spirit of God, depending on the Holy Spirit to guide and direct their past. This is the season East Gate believers are empowered with spiritual blessings (gifts, talents) to bear the purpose and will of God through the power of God's might. The East Gate is a place where believers are rejoicing in giving and being used by God to further the Kingdom of God. This is the season when East Gate believers are emptying themselves of the gospel of Jesus Christ, holding back nothing. This is a season when East Gate believers are constantly fighting the good fight of faith for others as spiritual midwives.

The East Gate is a time when the believer stands unwavering in the truth of God's word because of His faithfulness. This is a place where believers consider their ways regarding their relationship with Christ, their spiritual growth, their ability to reproduce the likeness of Christ. This is the gate where believers are accounting for God's investment in their lives, accounting for the people God places in their care, accounting for the returns on God's gifts, talents, power, and promises to edify the body of Christ and tell the story that Jesus is Lord.

This is the phase of the metamorphosis when the believer's prayer life increases greatly. The East Gate believer begins watching and praying for those lost, those who haven't made the decision to accept the general or effectual calling making Jesus the Lord over their life. This is a time the East Gate believer feasts on the word of God day and night, sounding the alarm to anyone who has ears to hear what the Spirit of the Lord is saying. This is a place where the believer's hope of salvation is unfaltering, and the promise of eternal life is imminent. This is the gate where believers are standing tall and looking good, taking earnest heed to the gospel of Jesus Christ, rooted and grounded with the mind of Christ.

This is a time when East Gate believers are well grounded in their faith, no space to turn back, have no confidence in the flesh but hold on to the hope of their salvation. This is the season and place where East Gate believers are establishing good discipline and stability in their faith that stands against the infinite wisdom of this world and its systems. This is the season when East Gate believers are rooted, grounded, and built up in Christ abounding therein with thanksgiving.

This is the season East Gate believers are operating in their spiritual gifts, enriched (fertile, productive) in Christ Jesus. This is the gate where believers exercise divine insight into the faith, constantly seeking the depth, width, length, and height of the love of God. The East Gate is where believers are experiencing an endless love through a personal experience with Christ. This is the season when East Gate believers are identified with Christ, blameless and beyond reproach, watching for His appearance. This is the gate where believers' unflinching endurance exercises the firmness in their faith with patience eagerly awaiting the hope of their salvation. This is the season the East Gate believer is alert (active in faith), having knowledge of Jesus's appearance yet laboring as if today is the day of the consummation of their salvation. This is the season East Gate believers remain ready (active power that works within believers) to rejoice at His appearance with a clear conscience, clean hands, and a pure heart. This is the season when East Gate believers are feeding God's lambs and sheep with the spiritual growth food source (word of God) as directed by the Holy Spirit.

This is the season when believers who serve as eyewitnesses of God's majesty, looking for and hasting unto Jesus's appearance for His church. The East Gate is a place where believers position themselves viewing the glass as half full seeking God's goodness. The East Gate is where believers are digging deep in the knowledge of God and laying their foundation on the cornerstone (Jesus) for sustainment. This is the season the East Gate believer is no longer seeking affirmation from mankind to avoid fear of persecution but receiving the righteousness of God through faith. This is the season when believers are aware that the shared blood of Jesus accepted by God is more than enough to validate the believer's salvation.

This is the season when believers have mastered the Dung Gate experience, having managed the desires of the flesh through the light of the gospel of Jesus Christ. This is the gate where believers demonstrate Jesus's First Discourse (Sermon of the Mount) by showing themselves merciful, displaying a spirit of meekness, taking on the challenge to be the salt of the earth and the light of the world, standing as the peacemaker exemplifying the effectual calling of God. This is the phase of the complete metamorphosis when the East Gate believers recognize they stand in the presence of God because of His grace. The East Gate is a season when the believer is holding fast the name of Jesus and their faith awaiting His appearance. The East Gate reminds believers of Jesus's appearance for His church. This return of Jesus for His church is the promise of God, "hope of glory fulfilled," to be in the presence of God forever. East Gate believers are fully persuaded with confident and earnest expectation (based on God's word), knowing that they have been changed from faith to faith being conformed in the image of Jesus the Christ. It is the Christ in the believer that upholds the believer's legal spiritual rights to share in Jesus's glory. At Jesus's return, East Gate believers will see Him as he is face to face (crowned with glory and honor). The East Gate is where believers understand the grace of God and His love, for the body of Christ propels them to live their lives understanding Jesus's first coming and has made it easy to rest in their hope for his second appearance. So, then, East Gate believers are ready for Jesus's appearance with earnest hope that when He appears, they will be with Him for eternity. Believers that wait on the Lord (in service, acting on their profession of faith in His absence) shall renew their strength (studying the word of God to show themselves approval, redeeming the times); they shall not be weary of Jesus's appearance. Believers are charged to spread the good news that Jesus died on a cross and rose again, and when He appears, those that are asleep in Jesus will God bring with him. East Gate believers will be caught up together in the clouds to meet the Lord in the air, and so shall they be with the Lord. East Gate believers are charged to comfort one another with these words. This is a time when East Gate believers will rejoice in Jesus's appearance, having no need to strike the lintel and the side posts with blood, nor bind a line of scarlet thread in the windows of their lives. Jesus knows His sheep. East Gate believers are to discern the times knowing that no man, no angels, and not even the Son of Man knows the day or the hour of His appearance, therefore be warned and be prepared.

Can you say with confidence that your faith and faithfulness toward God is purehearted? Will you be able to stand in the presence of His appearance with joy and excitement? Will your faithfulness to God's calling for your life receive the praise of a faithful servant? Will your gifts and talents find you a faithful servant, or will your works be counted among the slothful and wicked servants? It is my prayer that your earnest expectation and excitement regarding Jesus's appearance warm your heart knowing that your faithfulness toward the calling of God for your life is fulfilled.

The Inspection Gate: Gathering of the Redeemer and the Redeemed

The Inspection Gate is an event that has not happened yet. Therefore, this chapter will use biblical scriptures to draw the conclusion that Christ (bridegroom) will make an appearance to receive his bride (ecclesia: believers that have been called out of the world). The Inspection Gate is designed to review the works and faithfulness of believers toward God. The believer's faithfulness toward the purpose and plan of God for their lives will be at the forefront for accountability. The believer will be required to give an account for their deeds (good or bad) and faithfulness toward God.

The Inspection Gate reminds believers of gathering the troops for numbering and inspection or examination. The Inspection Gate is the pinnacle of all the gates. The Inspection Gate has a military connotation pertaining to the gathering of the troops for an inspection. This inspection is Jesus's appearance to gather believers identified by the indwelling Spirit of the living God. The concern with this inspection is the timing and unannounced formality of its proceedings. Preparation at the Inspection Gate can be prolonged, as no one knows the day, or the hour God the Father will release the Son of God to change his posture and go retrieve his bride. This is the last gate before returning to the Sheep Gate, as Jesus is Alpha and Omega. The bible states, "For the Lord himself shall descend from heaven with a shout, with the voice of the archangel, and with the trump of God: and the dead in Christ shall rise first: Then we which are alive and remain shall be caught up together with them in the clouds, to meet the Lord in the air: and so, shall we ever be with the Lord." The Son of Man (in his deity) will come to gather his bride (the Church) to review their faithfulness in preparation for rewards. In preparation for the bridegroom's coming, the bride is directed by the written covenant and union between God and the believer to put on the newness of life. The Son of Man (Jesus Christ) will be the presiding official over this inspection.

The believer (bride) has accepted the effectual calling (marriage proposal) to prepare themselves for the day that God the Father will direct His Son to go and consummate the marriage. The bride has been working hard to put off anything that goes against their covenant agreement with God the Father (word of

God). The bride of Christ (Church) has put on a veil for the wedding symbolizing her commitment to the bridegroom, acknowledging rejection of the world's systems, purity, innocence, and virginity. The veil (bridal ensemble) is to be removed only by the bridegroom to symbolize modesty and intimacy between the bride and the bridegroom. This veil is a public proclamation before God that the believer loves the bridegroom and desires to make Him Lord over their lives. The bride has put on Christ, put on the armor of light making no provisions for their flesh, put on the new man which is renewed in knowledge after the image of the bridegroom, put on the elect of God the Father, prepared to put on incorruption and immortality and most of all love. When Jesus returns, he will find the bride having experienced all the gates and spiritual growth to ensure the marriage is equally yoked. This is the bride (believer) who has not defiled their garment with the smut of the world's systems. This is the believer who, when standing before the Judgment Seat of Christ (Bema Seat), let the record show that this believer hungers and thirst after righteousness; this believer remains sober and watchful for the bridegroom's appearance. This is the bride who is constantly being cleansed by the power of the word of God. This is the bride who has put off the deeds of the old man, overcoming the cares of this world to ensure they have not defiled their garment. This is the bride who continues without ceasing the work of faith, labor of love, and patience of hope in Jesus Christ. The Inspection Gate announces, "the marriage of the Lamb" and warns the bride regarding their garment to be prepared to meet the bridegroom. The bride is to "put on their beautiful garments," fine linen, clean and white, which symbolizes the righteousness of the saints. The bride (believer) is required to be spiritually clothed in the wedding articles (garment of salvation and the robe of righteousness) to fulfill the covenant agreement. These spiritual coverings signify the redemptive blood of Jesus Christ as the lamb of God. The garment (dress code) suited for the appearance of the bride for His bridegroom is identified by its spiritual covering (garment of salvation and the robe of righteousness). These spiritual coverings are likened unto the wind; one can see the effect of the wind and hear the wind but cannot tell whether it is coming or going (pneuma: breath of life). Likewise, this spiritual covering has side effects that can be viewed by mankind, but the source of its effects is spiritually discerned. The Inspection Gate believers are confident in their spiritual covering prepared by God (as a potter) to protect and defend against the wiles of the enemies of this world. God does this by building hedges around his bride, entertaining them in the secret place of the most high for their comfort. God's rod and staff comfort the believer with grace, power, authority, and glory as the Inspection Gate believer rejoices at Jesus's appearance. This is the kind of covering where the goodness of God overshadows the Inspection Gate believer with the covering of the almighty God. This is the season the Inspection Gate believer delights in the gospel of Jesus Christ experiencing the results of a tree planted by rivers of living waters.

The Hebrew word for covering is to conceal or hide something entirely from view. The Inspection Gate believer understands that they have been crucified with Christ and the Spirit that dwells in the believer has lordship over their lives. The Inspection Gate believer is hidden in Christ, as He now lives in the believer with total Lordship (by choice) in the life of the believer. The Inspection Gate believer by faith is completely immersed (baptized) in Christ out of the world's view (mankind's physical attributes to see the unseen).

I'm reminded of the parable in which the Kingdom of Heaven is like unto a certain king, who made a marriage for his son, and sent his servant to call them that were bidden (invited) to the wedding. The servants were directed to go to the highways and byways to find them that were bidden (invited, ordered, commanded) to the marriage. The voice of many waters, the voice of a great multitude, and the voice of a mighty thundering ushered the king into the wedding chamber to officiate the wedding of his son. The king came into the assembly to officiate the marriage and recognized a guest that was not covered with the proper wedding garment (God's grace, garment of salvation and the robe righteousness) that was provided for them. The king instructed the servants to bind them (he who rejected His Son) and carry him to the outer darkness where there is weeping and gnashing of teeth.

The word of God is clear that the ungodly shall not stand in judgment nor in the congregation of the righteous. Mankind cannot come before a holy God dressed in their own good works of righteousness. The best righteousness mankind can muster is as filthy rages in His presence. The redemptive blood cleaning is evidence of the Inspection Gate believer's ethical conduct, moral courage, integrity, faithfulness, and godly character. If the grace of God, the Spirit of God, is not recognized by the officiating officer (Son of Man) at His appearance, then you are not invited to the wedding.

The Inspection Gate (Judgment Seat of Christ) does not have anything to do with determining the believer's salvation; the believer's salvation was determined by the work of Christ on the cross. There is no judgment for sin to those in Christ Jesus. This is the grace of God, that God has chosen not to remember the bride's sin. The Inspection Gate will speak to the Judgment Seat of Christ, and the day of consummation of the hope of the believer's salvation and eternal life. The Judgment Seat of Christ is not a judgment for condemnation, but a tribunal court for rewards. The word of God has made it crystal clear that there is no condemnation to those in Christ Jesus. This inspection of the soldiers of God has to do with believers giving an account for the gifts, talents, anointing, and provisions provided by God to edify the body of Christ; to feed God's lambs, to feed God's sheep and expand the Kingdom of God. The inspection checklist is geared toward the believer's faithfulness toward God as it pertains to the gifts and talents provided by God to the believer for His purpose and the believer's good works and faithful service. The checklist for this inspection cannot be exclusive, as God (word of God) is unsearchable.

There are many prophecies regarding the first coming of the Messiah (the anointed one) fulfilled in Jesus Christ. Each of these prophecies requires believers to have experienced the Sheep Gate (indwelling of the Holy Spirit) to recognize Jesus in these prophecies. The prophets in the Old Testament

Bible spoke Jesus into existence by making sure every nation knew that a savior was coming that would take away the sin(s) of this world. The prophets of the Old Testament Bible provided prophecies that leave no doubt that the seed of woman would come from the tribe of Judah to take away the sins of the world.

Likewise, the followers of Christ have become the New Testament covenant prophets, warning and alerting the world that this same Jesus would return for His church to ensure His bride (Church) would escape the day of trouble. The day of trouble has been identified as a day of destruction from the almighty, as a day of darkness and gloominess, as a day of clouds and thick darkness. The prophet Zechariah identifies the sight of Jesus's second coming at the Mount of Olives. The gospel of Matthew declares that the sign of the Son of Man will appear in the sky with great power and glory, and every eye shall see Him. The pastor Titus teaches believers to deny ungodliness and worldly lust while awaiting the blessed hope and glorious appearing of Jesus Christ. Those who ignored the gospel of Jesus Christ and entered not by the Sheep Gate will view Jesus's second coming as the greatest calamity in all of history. It is appointed unto mankind once to die, but after death judgment.

Appearance of the Bridegroom (Jesus Christ)

The prophecies of the first coming of the Messiah fulfilled in Jesus Christ were not enough for many nations to recognize Jesus as the Lamb of God that would take away the sins of the world. Jesus's first coming was met with doubt, partly because according to mankind's expectation based on their own checklist (righteousness), Jesus didn't make the cut. Even after Jesus's ministry, many miracles, and teachings that the Kingdom of God was at hand, many did not believe.

Likewise, the Lamb of God has been crucified for the sins of the world reconciling mankind to God; Jesus has risen from the grave with all power in His hands; the Holy Spirit and the grace of God is available to whomsoever will believe, yet many don't believe. The new covenant ambassadors of Christ are preaching and teaching that Jesus will make an appearance to receive His own. The gospel of the Kingdom of God and the epistles (New Testament) have provided signs and events of His appearance for believers to take hold and have an attitude of rejoicing at His appearance.

I'm reminded of the scripture in the book of Acts where the Apostle Paul speaks to the relationship between Jesus and his chosen few. Jesus the Christ shows Himself alive on many occasions to many different nations of people. Jesus's chosen few witnesses spoke to Him asking Him a question regarding the restoring of the Kingdom of Israel. Jesus replied, "It is not for you to know the times or the seasons, which the Father has put in his own power." Afterward Jesus was taken up (ascended) and a cloud received him out of their sight. Standing by were two messengers of God dressed in white apparel, comforting the witnesses, saying, "This same Jesus shall come again in the same manner you see him go."

The message to believers from the fivefold ministry regarding the Inspection Gate is do not doubt, God is not a man that He can lie, His word is final. The message to believers is do not cast away your confidence and patience established in the Valley Gate. These spiritual forces (patience and confidence) will propel believers to do the will of God while waiting on His return. The appearance of Jesus Christ is the blessed hope of believers that God is faithful to his promises and prophecies of His word. Jesus's first coming as the Messiah (suffering savior) fulfilled many of prophecies during his birth, life, ministry, death, and resurrection; however, his return for his Church (bride) will fulfill the hope of salvation and eternal life for believers. God is not a man that He should lie; His word has made it clear that "it is appointed unto man once to die and then the judgment." This event is not questionable nor debatable and will come to pass. This is the gate where believers gird up their lions and push out their chests, having completed the spiritual transformation. This is the season when believers are standing tall before the Lord of Lords and the King of Kings with clean hands and pure hearts. This is the season believers are resting in the Belt of Truth (gospel of Jesus Christ) knowing that Jesus will return for them, and they shall be with Him forever. The word of God regarding Jesus's appearance for His bride has been promised by Jesus Himself.

Day of Consummation for Believers

The day of consummation (completion) is the official day of the inspection officiated by the Son of Man. The Inspection Gate believer has begotten a lively hope resourced by God's abundant mercy and the resurrection of Jesus Christ from the dead. This lively hope is reserved in the presence of God as an inheritance for those that believe and hold fast to His word. A lively hope is an active hope seeing the unseen based on God's promises written in His word.

A lively hope is the kind of hope that settles the desire of the heart of the believer for faith (evidence) of the unseen desire(s) to surely come to pass. The day of consummation will reveal the believer's salvation and hope of eternal life. This day of hope and faith will culminate (come to an end) the promises of God's word being fulfilled at Jesus's appearance. This is the day of the hope of the believer's salvation that they will receive at the end of their faith to include salvation for their soul. This day of consummation is where the grace of God will overshadow all who have confidence and are fully persuaded that the Spirit of God that dwells in believers will reveal the suffering of Christ and the glory that should follow at His appearance.

Inspection Gate believers understand that they are partakers of Christ's suffering as they enter into the victory that He has accomplished for His bride on the cross. Believers have been empowered to stand against the wiles of the enemies of this world; believers have the authority to cast down imaginations and anything that comes against the word of God. Inspection Gate believers deny one's self the appetites and desires of the flesh experienced in the Dung Gate; Inspection Gate believers have fought a good fight of faith in the Horse Gate, all because the believer exercised their rights as joint heirs with Christ. The day of consummation will reveal the believers' suffering as partakers in Christ's sacrifice (passion) which solidifies the believer's salvation. The word of God declares that such trials and tribulations are honorable, profitable, and considered light afflictions of the glory to be revealed at His appearance. The Inspection Gate believer's hope is steadfast, knowing their inheritance as partakers of His suffering, and they shall be also of the consolation (comfort, sympathy, compassion).

I'm reminded of the scripture in First Corinthians where the gift of love is expressed by the Apostle Paul. Paul tells believers that after Jesus's ascension there remains faith, hope, and charity (love) in this age. Faith is defined as the assurance (evidence) of things hoped for or the conviction of something not seen by mankind's physical attributes. Hope has a totally different meaning and is not to be confused with a wish. A wish has its strength in the desire of the person that wishes. Earnest hope (lively hope) or biblical hope provides a positive expectation, as their hope is based on the promises of God and His strength and faithfulness.

Believers' labor and faithfulness toward God expresses their love for God who apprehended them for His purpose. The day of consummation will allow believers to stand before the Judgment Seat of Christ rejoicing, knowing their labor has not been in vain.

God's Concerns for the Church (Bride)

The Inspection Gate checklist cannot be exclusive, and any attempt to solicit a list by which the Son of Man will judge the believer would be pointless. However, the churches in the book of Revelation provide some serious concerns of Jesus the Christ that drew His presence for correction. If the Church (body of Christ) is going to stand tall at Jesus's appearance at the Inspection Gate, they should take heed to these issues.

The Church at Ephesus describes a believer (Church) that labors to do good works. A believer who has established patience, humility, and fights against the evildoers with a passion. These are the believers who are working in the Kingdom of God and in the body of Christ, maybe even in the fivefold ministry (apostles, prophets, evangelists, pastors, and teachers). These believers are constantly laboring in the name of Jesus Christ with great zeal. The life of this believer appears to be holy and consecrated to God as a faithful servant. The scripture defines a faithful servant as one who obeys the commandments of God. The Ephesus believer's standard of life is based on the world's definition of success and is sought after by religious folks.

The issue God has with this believer is their intent and motives of their good works, whether their good works are linked to the purpose and plan of God through the works of the Holy Spirit or works of the flesh. This is the believer who does not understand or has forgotten their union agreement with Christ (the branch cannot bear fruit of itself) at the expense of losing the leadership of the head of the Church (Christ). This believer has lost or forgotten their first love (God). They seem to have forgotten when they were neophytes in the Fish Gate evangelizing the Kingdom of God solely because of their love for God. This is the believer (Church) who has positioned Jesus at the table of their lives in their peripheral vision for counseling, instead of at the head of the table. John 4:19: "We love him, because he first loved us." The Ephesus believers are working in the body of Christ to gain mankind's accolades, attention, or monetary gain and will find themselves disappointed and ashamed when standing at the Judgment Seat of Christ. When the flesh does good works in its own strength, there is no spiritual growth, there is no reward stored in heaven for these works. The results of fleshly good works will always find their genesis in selfishness. These works are rejected by God, as the flesh cannot please God. God is love, and without love (God) the acts of mankind apart from God are nothing more than a sounding brass or a tinkling cymbal profiting nothing.

If this is you: When the presence of the Son of Man (He that holdeth the seven stars in His right hand, who walketh in the midst of the seven golden candlesticks) chastises you, have ears to hear what the Spirit of the Lord is saying. God directs this believer to remember where they have fallen short of the glory of God. God directs this believer to realign themselves with His plan and provision. This belief is directed to return to their first love, understanding that nothing can separate God's love from them.

If the union with Christ is going to bring forth fruit accepted by God, believers will be required to abide in Christ. The Ephesus believer is charged to examine themselves and realize their works are in vain and their sacrifice(s) are rejected by God. God directs this believer to repent. To turn back to Him through the counseling of the Holy Spirit. Then, the believer is to return to doing the agreed-upon work of God to further His kingdom through the works of the Holy Spirit.

The Church at Pergamos is the believer (Church) that appears not to be moved by the things of this world and the change in culture. This is the believer who will tell others that they have the "old-school faith," stating, "If God said it, I believe it and that settles it." This is the believer who proclaims that they are sold out to the gospel of the Kingdom of God and not willing to deny Jesus in any space they find themselves. The life of this believer looks good on paper and in the eyes of the world. This is the believer who has gained monetary status, attends church regularly, and gives financially. This is the believer who boasts regarding their giving to the Church and its purpose and how God has established houses for their comfort and has blessed them with worldly possessions.

The issue God has with this believer is the stumbling blocks they put in the way of anyone who threatens their position and reputation in their local ministry. This is the believer or ministry that has no discernment of the Spirit of God, nor fear of rejecting God's message or messenger. "You can't preach in this ministry until voted in by the church leaders." "In order to join this ministry, the congregation is required to provide a unanimous vote." These stumbling blocks are designed to teach outsiders their gospel, their god(s). This is the believer who worships God with their lips, but their heart is far from the truth. This is the believer who esteems themselves above others by persecuting other believers for their shortcomings. This is the believer or ministry that changes the word of God to coincide with their way of life. This is the believer or ministry that teaches idols and changes the truth of God's word to stay relevant to a constantly changing culture to keep the congregation intact for monetary purposes. This is the believe who has changed the truth of God's word into a lie and worshipped and served the creature more than the creator. "It's okay for a man to have affections for another man." "You can't help who or whom you love." Therefore, conjuring themselves in ministry rituals of false teaching that support and harbor these idols and ideas. Additionally, this is the ministry that has established layers of leadership that support their doctrine as senior advisors over babes in Christ (laity).

If this is you: When Jesus Christ (He which hath the sharp sword with two edges) comes to reproof, correct, purify your soul, take heed. God's warning for this believer is to repent immediately and should not be ignored! The Water Gate experience has provided the weapon of choice to cut through these doctrines and establish the true doctrine to present to God's people. Repent now (immediately) and ask God for forgiveness.

The Church at Thyatira is a believer or ministry who has taken God's greatest commandment by storm, and their service, faith, patience, love, and good works have continued to grow under the power of the almighty God. This is the believer who is committed to God's purpose and plan for their lives, loyal and powerless in their own strength, depending and relying on God for their next breath.

The issue God has with this believer is they allow false teaching in their presence to seduce God's people to believe fornication or sex is not a sin. This is the believer or ministry who has allowed a Jezebel's spirit to have access to the teaching of God's people, seducing the people of God to commit fornication. This is the believer that will be held accountable for standing by and doing nothing to correct this false teaching. Believers are charged to become God's watchmen, salt of the earth, and the light of the world. "So, thou, O son of man, I have set thee a watchman unto the house of Israel; therefore, thou shalt hear the word at my mouth, and warn them for me." The word of God reminds believers that if the watchman sees the corruption that comes against the word of God and does not blow the trumpet and warn the people, the destruction and damage from this corruption God will require at the hand of the watchman. Jude the brother of James said, "There are certain men crept in unawares, who were before of old ordained to this condemnation, ungodly men, turning the grace of our God into lasciviousness (lustful things of this world), and denying Jesus Christ."

If this is you: When the Son of God (who hath His eyes like unto a flame of fire, and His feet are like fine brass) pricks your heart of these serious turns of events, repent. Remove yourself from this teaching or be a voice for God to warn and alert false doctrine as the extension of Jesus Christ on earth.

The Church at Sardis is a believer that believes within themselves they are doing the will of God for their life and working hard in their local church and community to lift up the name of Jesus. This is the believer whose outer garment and lifestyle appear to be linked to the gospel of the Kingdom of God. This is the believer who is yet a babe in Christ and is afraid or too prideful to seek God and rather be counted among the religious leadership than to become naked and ashamed before God. This is the believer who appears to have been blessed by God in every area of their lives. This is the believer who "talks the talk" regarding the Kingdom of God only to be accepted by "church folks."

The issue God has with this believer is they have hardened their hearts and have become insensitive. The Holy Spirit is unable to convict this believer of their wrongdoings. This is the believer who has rejected the lifeline of the Holy Spirit and therefore can only produce dead works, as the Holy Spirit has no influence in this believer's way of life. This is the believer without the counseling of the Holy Spirit by choice. This is the believer who believes they have need for nothing, yet are wretched, miserable, poor, blind, and naked.

If this is you: When the Holy Spirit (He that hath the seven Spirits of God, and the seven stars) apprehends your presence, repent. It is the Holy Spirit that makes believers alive and viable for God's use. Without the Holy Spirit's presence and influence in the believer's life, the believer is of no use to anyone. If this conduct continues, the believer's conscience may become seared, spiritually complacent, and spiritually weak, leaving the believer to the dictates of the edicts of this world. Believers can only glorify God when their behavior, conduct, and fruit of their labor align with the likeness of God and the image of Jesus Christ.

The Church at Laodiceans is the believer who proclaims Jesus as their Lord and Savior but rejects the Lordship. This is the believer in which the Holy Spirit lies dormant and cannot show Himself strong in the believer's life for change. This is the believer that has no fear of God. This the believer who is straddling the fence between God and the world. This is the believer that praises and worships God on Sunday and allows the flesh to easily be troubled on Monday. This is the believer who habitually disobeys the indwelling of the Holy Spirit for their lustful desires. This is the believer who destroys and hurts others for their own gain and yet claims they are a child of God when convenient (fitting in well with their needs, activities, and plans). This is a lukewarm believer controlled by the enemy of this world and brings shame to the body of Christ, providing doubt to those lost and seeking God.

The issue God has with this believer is they are neither cold nor hot regarding God's purpose and plan for their lives. There is no earnest fear of God or passion toward God. The spiritual encounter with Jesus in the Sheep Gate was not followed up with evangelizing their position with Christ in the Fish Gate; their proclamation in the Fish Gate was not confirmed with evidence in the Valley Gate. This believer demonstrates no evidence of a successful Valley Gate experience (fear of God). This believer's heart is not clear (double-minded) and has no full commitment to the gospel of Jesus Christ. This is the believer whose heart is not settled and cannot glorify God nor be trusted with the gospel and the power thereof.

If this is you: When Jesus the Anointed One (the Amen, the faithful and true witness, the beginning of the creation of God) speaks to your heart, repent immediately. God commands this believer to put off the old nature and put on the new nature, making way for the discernment of the Spirit to be engaged in their lives.

Spiritual Growth

The spiritual transformation is complete. The Inspection Gate connects the temple walls from the Sheep Gate (Jesus Christ) to the Sheep Gate. Jesus is Alpha and Omega. The Inspection Gate has not happened yet; however, through the word of God, we can rest assured that Jesus will return for His bride (believers). Believers' faithfulness toward God is vital to rejoicing at Jesus's coming. The believer is excited at Jesus's coming because they have completed the spiritual metamorphosis and experienced each gate, and now rejoice at the Inspection Gate, which is the final gate.

The life of the believer is likened unto a race. All believers join an ongoing race at their acceptance in the beloved at the Sheep Gate. There are rules and laws that govern the race. There are rewards to be anticipated at the Inspection Gate while standing before the "Bema Seat" of Christ at His appearance. The rules are outlined in the word of God for all believers (runners) to adhere to. The rule for this race applies to all believers; however, the course for each runner can be very different. There is no need to judge others regarding their spiritual walk with Christ; we must all appear before the Judgment Seat of Christ, that everyone may receive their reward for their faithfulness toward God during their race. In preparation for this spiritual race, believers are to ensure the Belt of Truth (gospel of Jesus Christ) is available, active, and dominating the believer's thought process. In preparation for the inspection at the Inspection Gate, the believer is fully confident in their walk with God and their commitment and faithfulness to God in all their ways. The believer's Breastplate of Righteousness (truth realized that the believer is the righteousness of God) has freed the believer to spread the gospel with godly testimonies for their own strength and faith to whomever has ears to hear. The bride is making preparation to receive divine clothing from God that is appropriate for the wedding. This is the season the bride (believer) is clothed with the garments of salvation and covered with a robe of righteousness. The bride understands that being clothed in Christ is not a cloak to cover the believer's misery, but the believer is clothed with compassion, kindness, humility, meekness, and patience. The bride has put on the fruit of the Holy Spirit endowed with power from on high. This endowment sets the precedent regarding their position in Christ (joint heirs), their covenant agreement to follow after Christ, and their covenant agreement of God's blessing and protection promised to the faithful servants.

The bridegroom is decked with ornaments that

describe His splendor (majestic, dignity, honor) and His gaiety (rejoicing) as He comes out of His chamber. The bridegroom is ushered into the wedding as if it were the voice of a great multitude and as the voice of many waters, and as the voice of mighty thundering.

The bride has adorned herself with jewels that signify that the bride is to become a part of the bridegroom's extended family. The bridegroom and the bride are looking forward eagerly to the day of consummation.

The thought of having a deeper fellowship with the bridegroom after experiencing the spiritual metamorphosis escapes the Inspection Gate believer's mind. The joy to tell Jesus all about your troubles as if He didn't already know gives the bride goose bumps from the fear of His majesty and excitement of His appearance. The Inspection Gate believer is rejoicing in praise and worship at Jesus's coming for His bride. The Inspection Gate believer is found in Christ, not having his own righteousness but the righteousness which is of God by faith.

The Inspection Gate is a season when the believer has made preparation for the Award Banquet (Jesus's appearance) to receive the Crown of Righteousness, having accepted the effectual calling of God into the ministry of reconciliation in the Water Gate. This is the believer who has obeyed the written word of God (logos) and the spoken word of God (rhema word) as the Spirit of God gave utterance. This is the season believers are watching for the appearance of the bridegroom from the east. Second Timothy 4:8: "Henceforth there is laid up for me a crown of righteousness, which the Lord, the righteous judge, shall give me at that day: and not to me only, but unto all them also that love his appearing."

The Inspection Gate believer has made preparation to receive the Crown of Rejoicing after faithfully feeding God's lambs and sheep in the East Gate. This is a time when the Inspection Gate believer is looking forward to a place where there shall be no more death, nor sorrow, nor crying, and no more pain, for the former things have passed away and all things have become new. First Thessalonians 2:19: "For what is our hope, or joy, or crown of rejoicing? Are not even ye in the presence of our Lord Jesus Christ at his coming?"

The Inspection Gate believer has made preparation to receive the Crown of Life for their faithfulness endured in the Dung Gate experience having put away childish things, endured the temptation of the flesh obeying the word of God. James 1:12: "Blessed is the man that endureth temptation: for when he is tried, he shall receive the crown of life, which the Lord hath promised to them that love him."

The Inspection Gate believer has made preparation to receive the Crown of Glory. This is the time when the believer is excited regarding Jesus's appearance, waiting and anticipating the brightness of His glory revealed in the Valley Gate experience. This is the bride that is a witness of the suffering of Christ and is a partaker of the glory that shall be revealed. First Peter 5:1-4: "The elders which are among you I exhort, who am also an elder, and a witness of the sufferings of Christ, and also a partaker of the glory that shall be revealed: ² Feed the flock of God which is among you, taking the oversight thereof, not by constraint, but willingly; not for filthy lucre, but of a ready mind; ³ Neither as being lords over God's heritage, but being examples to the flock. ⁴ And when the Chief Shepherd shall appear, ye shall receive a crown of glory that fadeth not away."

The Inspection Gate believer has made preparation to receive the Incorruptible Crown, having been faithful to the word of God putting on temperament (changed nature) and walking in the newness of life found in the Fountain Gate experience. First Corinthians 9:25: "And every man that striveth for the mastery is temperate in all things. Now they do it to obtain a corruptible crown; but we an incorruptible."

The Inspection Gate believer has taken off the shackles of self-dependency that once fastened their hands, so that God could love them, so that God could provide for their needs, so that God could give them all of Himself.

Are you ready to meet the Son of Man (Immanuel)? The Son of Man will come for His bride who is without spot and blameless before God (those accepted in the beloved). The Inspection Gate (bridegroom and the bride) is the assembly of the redeemed with the redeemer.

The Inspection Gate believer will reveal the likeness of God and the image of Christ. Act now to fill your horns with oil (the water of life and the Holy Spirit), clothe yourself with the fruit of the Spirit of God (humility, love, joy, peace, long-suffering, gentleness, goodness, faith, meekness, temperance), and be ready when the Son of Man comes. Accept the effectual calling of God for your life and become a living sacrifice for the expansion of the Kingdom of God. May the grace of Jesus Christ be with your spirit. Amen.

Acknowledgments

Many thanks to my wonderful wife, Marilyn Riley. Marilyn is the evidence of God's grace and might in our marriage, family, and extended family. Marilyn's relentless nurturing, caring, and encouraging growth and development of others can only be accomplished through Christ. Marilyn, only God loves you more.

Many thanks to Mr. Joseph Brassfield, my editor, earthly counselor, and friend. Many thanks to Mr. Gregory Booth and Mr. Bill Hammonds for their friendship, encouragement, time, and patience as sounding boards for the message and messenger of this book.

About the Author

The author, Ralph Riley, is one of eight boys born to parents of sharecroppers in a small Florida town. His parents held unwavering faith and diligence while working hard to provide the necessities of life for their family. The content of this book impregnated him long ago but didn't make haste to release its wisdom. He is grateful and beholden that God would use him to reveal his power over all the power of the enemy.

www.ingramcontent.com/pod-product-compliance
Lightning Source LLC
Chambersburg PA
CBHW050225100526
44585CB00017BA/2016